Also by G. Shields:

THIRD EDITION: READY FOR YOUR CLOSE UP? AFRICAN AMERICANS AND INTERNATIONALS IN CINEMA WHO ARE COLLEGE GRADUATES- EXPANDED HONORABLE MENTION EDITION

RAP TO CINEMA

Hip Hop Music Artists Who Cross Over to Film

by G. Shields

Profiles of rap artists who transition into multifaceted areas of filmmaking: acting, writing, directing, and producing.

 POSITIVE PROGRESSION PUBLISHER

RAP TO CINEMA

Hip Hop Music Artists Who Cross Over to Film

Copyright © 2021

by G. Shields. All rights reserved.

No part of this publication may be reproduced, stored in a retrieval system, or transmitted in any way by any means, electronic, mechanical, photocopy, recording, or otherwise without the prior permission of the author except as provided by USA copyright law.

This book is designed to provide accurate and authoritative information concerning the subject matter covered. This information is given with the understanding that neither the author nor Positive Progression Publisher is engaged in rendering legal, professional advice. Since the details of your situation are fact-dependent, you should additionally seek the services of a competent professional.

Book design copyright © 2021 Cover design by G. Shields
Graphic Art & Logo Design: Sheryl Rhoades
Formatted by: Vision Novels

Published in the United States of America:
ISBN: 978-0-578-84485-5

Includes bibliography and index

1. Performing Arts / Film & Music/ Reference

2. Reference / Biographical Dictionaries

DARE TO TURN ADVERSITY INTO ADVANTAGE

You can be the phenomenal ancestor/individual whose shoulders the future stands on

CONTENTS

Introduction..vii

Role of Actor, Producer, Director, Screenwriter
Cinematographer and Independent Filmmaker........................ 1

Rap/Film/Profiles..3

Rap to Cinema Honorable Mention..55

Honorable Mention (continued from) *Third Edition:
Ready For Your Close Up? African Americans And
Internationals In Cinema Who Are College Graduates*.................56

List of Hip Hop/Rap Movies (Select)..57

Bibliography..63

Index..67

INTRODUCTION

Rap music represents more of hip hop culture than dance, fashion and art combined. No one could have imagined the worldwide influence and impact rap music would have when introduced in 1970's Bronx, NY. All genres of film and television are quick to embrace rap as a soundtrack and apply the artistry of a rapper's skills to acting, producing, and writing. The role of rap's music and film contribution, singularly and combined, has contributed tremendously to the economy and livelihood of members engaged in both art forms. No doubt, rap music has benefitted greatly as a result of unparalleled exposure via film, television, and the internet. Rap's diverse rhythms of jazz, rhythm & blues, classical, Latin and more compliment an array of multimedia platforms.

Rap evolved from being sidelined to being an accepted musical genre recognized by mainstream and special interest awards. Contrary to negative rap lyrics, there are artists such as Will Smith who stated there is "no curse in my verse." Rap can be poetic and prolific when delving into life circumstances. Many rap artists record a clean or edited alternative to profane laced and sexually explicit version. There is soul-stirring gospel rap, as well.

Although rap artists are known to go on record and proclaim, they are not role models; they are. Young impressionable minds look to their poetic example as a way of creative expression and a pathway to success.

A point can be gotten across without constant (or no) profanity. The same goes for berating women and perpetrating violence. It's about contributing to and creating an upgraded reality. All forms of mass communication; movies, books, theatre, television, and video, can take heed. Create a reality where the best part of the message can be heard, processed, and accepted by all. Wider acceptance converts into more sales and opportunities.

The issue with the 'N' word, curse words, and derogatory betrayal of women cannot be overlooked, and need to be 'checked'. The National Association For The Advancement Of Colored People (NAACP) official position on the 'N' word is: "Therefore, be it resolved that the National Association for the Advancement of Colored People shall not condone, award, or engage any person that uses the N-word in any capacity, or in any artistic endeavor that does not allude to the historical context of the word, or that does not highlight the prejudicial nature of the word."

The NAACP resolution goes on to encourage members to ban the use of the N-word and bolster education and awareness about the offensiveness of the word across racial and generational lines through community outreach and public awareness.

Rap music has been a catalyst for many artists' transition to film and television. For artists such as Queen Latifah, LL Cool J, Ice Cube, Eve, Bow Wow, Niki Minaj, MC Hammer, Common, T.I., and countless others able to navigate the transition, stardom went from mega to stratospheric.

The criterion for the rap artists profiled in this book is an established relationship to cinema. Rap musicians have film soundtrack credits that include music projects that were recorded hits before being attached or included in a film or television project. For that reason, soundtrack and other music resumes are not listed. The focus for this topical reference book will be on the film resume. Television projects are listed only if cinema projects are included. Selected film projects and awards are mentioned.

The profiled artists are rappers who were able to apply their talent and work ethic to film. A recurring commonality among those profiled is the capability to protect the mind, respect the body, and develop a strong work ethic with time well spent in leisure activity while in pursuance of a never-ending quest for love and balance. The possession of strong entrepreneurial skills, philanthropy, and uplifting influence are well represented.

Historical Spotlight On

James Edwards (1918-1970), actor, film, and television writer. Edwards' shoulders are the shoulders every post-racial nonstereotyped person of African origin in the film industry stands on. He broke barriers in role portrayal as a film actor, and as a writer for television. Edwards was born in Muncie, Indiana. He majored in psychology at Knoxville College in Tennessee and graduated from Northwestern University where he received a master's degree in drama. He financed his education, as so many Americans, after an honorable discharge from military service. During World War II, he was commissioned as a first lieutenant in the U.S. Army. After appearing on stage with the Federal Theatre Project and touring with the New York stage play, *Deep Are the Roots*, Edwards landed his first film acting role in 1949 as a prizefighter in the movie, The *Set-Up*. Of his many acting credits, he is most recognized for the lead role of soldier, Peter Moss in the movie *Home of the Brave* (1949), which deals with racial bigotry. In the 1950s and 1960s Edwards wrote television episodes for several popular series including Westinghouse Desilu Playhouse. John Drew Barrymore starred in his 1958 television play *Silent Thunder*. In 1980 Edwards was inducted into the Black Filmmakers Hall of Fame.

Movie (actor): *Legend of the Northwest* (1978), *Doomsday Voyage* (1972), *Patton* (1970), *Coogan's Bluff* (1968), T*he Young Runaways* (1968), *The Sandpiper* (1965), **The Manchurian Candidate** (1962), *Blood and Steel* (1959), *Pork Chop Hill* (1959), *Night of the Quarter Moon* (1959), *Anna Lucasta* (1958), *Tarzan's Fight for Life* (1958), *Fräulein* (1958), *Battle Hymn* (1957), *Men in War* (1957), *The Killing* (1956), *The Phenix City Story* (1955), *Seven Angry Men* (1955), *African Manhunt* (1955), *The Caine Mutiny* (1954, uncredited), *The Joe Louis Story* (1953), *The Member of the Wedding* (1952), *Bright Victory* (1951), *The Steel Helmet* (1951), *Manhandled* (1949, uncredited), *Home of the Brave* (1949), *The Set-Up* (1949)

Television (writer, credited): *Law of the Plainsmen* (1960, season 1, episode 26), *Westinghouse Desilu Playhouse* (1958, season 1, episode 6), *Fireside Theatre* (1954, season 7, episode 6)

Television (actor): A wide range of episodic appearances from 1953 to 1969

Selected Film Industry Position Descriptions

Actor: An actor is a person (performer) whose profession is acting on stage, in movies, or other forms of broadcast such as television, radio, internet, etc.

PRODUCERS, DIRECTORS, SCREENWRITERS, AND CINEMATOGRAPHERS

Behind the camera: producer, director, screenwriter, and cinematographer—the staple of cinema.

Producer: a person or group who provides funding and coordinates various aspects of creating an entertainment performance.

Executive Producer: responsible for financial investment.

Director: directs and controls the artistic making of a film and is responsible for the interpretive aspect.

Screenwriter: a person who writes scripts that are the dialogue and actions of a movie and other forms of graphic media, including television, video games, and comics.

Cinematographer: the profession of motion-picture photography; an artist who captures images electronically or on film through the use of visual recording.

INDEPENDENT FILMS: independent films are professional feature film productions usually produced on a minimal budget outside of the major film studio system.

Rap Artists' Film/Profiles

André 3000 aka André Benjamin (1975), rapper, singer, instrumentalist, actor, executive producer. Gracious and charismatic, Atlanta, Georgia-born André 3000's first major success is his collaboration in the musical duo OutKast. Teamed with Big Boi (Antwon Patton), he shared a major musical coup with the multi-award-winning album *Speakerboxx/The Love Below.* After eleven years strong in southern influenced hip hop, André 3000 made his first significant appearance onscreen in the 2003 film *Hollywood Homicide.* He put his producing skills to work in 2006 for the film *Idlewild* and executive produced the television series *Class of 3000.* André 3000 is quick to acknowledge that relationships and timing have just as much to do with success in the arts as talent. His creative contribution to cinema was recognized in 2006 at the Chicago International Film Festival with an award for Emerging Artist. By 2013, he played the lead role of Jimi Hendrix in *Jimi: All Is by My Side.*
Award: Grammy Award (2020, 2004, 2003, 2002, 2001), Chicago Film Festival (2006), American Music Award (2004, 2003)
Movie (producer and actor): *Idlewild,* (2006)
Movie (actor): *High Life* (2018), *Jimi: All Is by My Side* (2013), *Semi-Pro* (2008), *Battle In Seattle* (2007), *Charlotte's Web* (2006) *Revolver* (2005), *Four Brothers* (2005), *Be Cool* (2005), *Hollywood Homicide* (2003)
Television (actor, writer, music, executive producer): *Class of 3000* (2006-07)
Television (actor): *Dispatches from Elsewhere* (2020), *American Crime* (2016), *Dominique Belongs to Us* (2015, narrator), *The Shield* (2004 and 2008)

Big Boi aka Antwon Patton (1975), rapper, songwriter, record and movie producer, actor. Born in Savannah, Georgia; OutKast member, Big Boi stands out representing hip-hop's southern origin. He finds satisfaction in mentoring musical groups. Music first, Big Boi is open to continuing to pursue film ventures. In 2006

he proved he is a natural for acting in the role of Marcus in *ATL,* quickly followed by the musical *Idlewild,* in which he also produced and supervised the music. Big Boi has also appeared in roles on episodic television and movies made for television. In 2007 Black Reel Awards nominated him for Best Original Score for *Idlewild.*
Award: American Music Award (2004, 2003), Grammy Award (2004, 2003, 2002, 2001)
Movie (actor, producer, music supervisor): *Idlewild* (2006)
Movie (actor): *The Trap* (2019), *SuperFly* (2018), *How 2 Build a Rapper* (2008) *Who's Your Caddy?* (2007) *ATL* (2006)
Television Movie (actor): *The Bobby DeBarge Story* (2019), *The Cookout 2* (2011), *Freaknik: The Musical* (2010)
Television (actor): *Scream: The TV Series* (2019, Season 3, episode 4 and 5), *The Quad* (2018)

Big Daddy Kane aka Antonio Hardy (1968), rapper, actor, director. Big Daddy Kane is associated, significantly, with the golden age of hip hop which took place from the mid-1980s till the early 1990s. Born in Brooklyn, NY, the stage name Kane is an acronym for King Asiatic Nobody's Equal. He made a highly regarded entrance as an actor in the movie classic *Posse* in 1993. He co-directed *Movie Madness* with Phillip Penza, which was released in 2016. In 1990 Big Daddy Kane won a Grammy for a collaborative project with Quincy Jones for the single *Back on the Block* from the album by the same name. He earned a Grammy nomination for the hit single *I Get the Job Done,* as a solo artist in 1991.
Movie (director, actor): *Movie Madness* (2016)
Movie (actor): *I Need A Man* (2016), *Exposed* (2016), *My Name Is Nobody* (2014), *You're Nobody 'til Somebody Kills You* (2012), *Just Another Day* (2009), *Love for Sale* (2008), *Dead Heist* (2007), *The Meteor Man* (1993), *Posse* (1993)
Television (actor): *Law & Order: Special Victims Unit* (2018, season19, episode 21)

Big Pun aka Christopher Lee Rios (1971-2000), rapper, actor. Born in the Bronx borough of New York City, Big Pun was a self-educated avid reader who left home and school at age 15. He accomplished much in his twenty-eight years, including being the first Latin rap artist to have a certified platinum album as a solo act. The married father of three starred in his share of requisite music videos, and as an actor in film and television.
Movie (actor): *Thicker Than Water* (1999), *Whiteboyz* (1999)
Television (actor): *Moesha* (1998, season 4, episode 7)

Biz Markie aka Marcel Theo Hall (1964), rapper, comedian, producer, actor. Recognized for his ability to audibly beatbox early in his 'fun loving' rap career, Biz Markie blazed a versatile trail representing hip hop. With the phenomenal success of songs *The Vapors* in 1988 and *Just A Friend* in 1999, doors opened for him to utilize other talents. Born in New Jersey and raised in Long Island, New York, Biz Markie is a constant presence in film and television as an actor or performing on soundtracks. In between, he is on the road performing.
Movie (actor): *Men in Black II* (2002)
Television Movie (actor): *Sharknado 2: The Second One* (2014)
Television (actor, select): *Black-ish* (2017, season 3, episode 24), *Crank Yankers* (2004-2007, voice), *In Living Color* (1994)

Black Thought aka Tariq Trotter (1971), rapper, writer, actor, executive producer. A master rap artist and unequivocally the best in freestyle socially conscious rhyme, Black Thought is a native of Philadelphia, PA. With Questlove, he is one of the founding members of the hip hop band, The Roots. His talent for acting was initially tapped for a role in Spike Lee's *Bamboozled* in 2000. Black Thought starred in the highly acclaimed *Brooklyn Babylon* in 2001, in the role of Solomon. He stays busy appearing in numerous episodic television series, including a recurring role on *The Deuce* (2017). He rounded out major casting in the movie *Get on Up* (2014). In 2019, Black Thought stepped into the position of

executive producer for the television documentary *Hip Hop: The Songs That Shook America*.
Award (select, numerous awards won in collaboration with The Roots band): Grammy Award (2016, 2011, 2000), NAACP Image Award (2011, 2007)
Movie (actor): *Popstar: Never Stop Never Stopping* (2016), *Stealing Cars* (2015), *Brotherly Love* (2015), *Get on Up* (2014), *On the Inside* (2011), *Yelling to the Sky* (2011), *Night Catches Us* (2010), *Explicit ILLs* (2008), *Love Rome* (2004), *Brooklyn Babylon* (2001), *Bamboozled* (2000)
Documentary (executive producer): *40 Years a Prisoner* (2020), *Hip Hop: The Songs That Shook America* (2019)
Television (actor): *Random Acts of Flyness* (2018, season 1, episode 1), *The Deuce* (2017)

Busta Rhymes aka Trevor Smith, Jr. (1972), rapper, actor, video director. Brooklyn, New York native, Busta Rhymes is in the vanguard of starring in colorful, extravagant music video productions. Having appeared on television and cinematic films, he was ready to co-direct the *Put Your Hands Where My Eyes Could See* music video with Hype Williams and Irv Gotti. In 1999, teamed with Janet Jackson, Busta Rhymes took home The Source Award, Music Video of the Year for "*What's It Gonna Be?*" By 2000 his acting ability was given full range in the movies *Shaft* (2000) and *Finding Forester* (2000). As part of a production team, Busta Rhymes won an Online Film & Television Association Award in 2014 for his art design for the television miniseries *Fargo*.
Award: Online Film & Television Association Award (2014), BET Award (3 in 2011, 2002), BET Hip Hop Award (4 in 2011, 2006), Soul Train Award (2000), Source Award (1999)
Movie (actor): *King of the Dancehall* (2016), *The Unforgiven* (2011), *Full Clip* (2006), *Dude...We're Going To Rio* (2003), *Halloween: Resurrection* (2002), *Narc* (2002), *Finding Forester* (2000), *Shaft* (2000), *Higher Learning* (1995), *Who's The Man?* (1993)
Television Movie (actor): *Strapped* (1993)
Television (actor): *The Masked Singer* (2020)

Cam'ron aka Cameron Ezike Giles (1976), rapper, actor, producer. After an interest in basketball, New York-born Cam'ron successfully pursued music. Throughout his music and film projects, he has consistently teamed with rappers Jim Jones and Juelz Santana. For a while, they were all members of the rap group The Diplomats, founded by Freekey Zekey. Early in his music career, Cam'ron wrote hits for some of the most notable rap artists in the business, which includes Lil' Kim's song *Crush On You*. For the year 2006 one hundred and twenty-eight-minute video *Killa Season,* he served as the writer, executive producer, director, editor, and actor. Cam'ron made his first film appearance with a small role in the 2002 movie, *Paper Soldiers*.
Movie (writer, executive producer, director, actor): *Killa Season* (2006)
Video Documentary (co-producer): *Jim Jones: A Day in the Fast Life* (2008).
Movie (actor): *Honor Up* (2018), *Percentage* (2014), *State Property: Blood on the Streets* (2005), *Paid in Full* (2002), *Paper Soldiers* (2002)

Childish Gambino aka Donald Glover (1983), rapper, writer, actor, musician, comedian, executive producer, director. Glover's diverse talent is strong in each category. He admirably showcases African dance moves tinged with modern during music performances, as demonstrated in the *This Is America* (2018) video. Having made a fortuitous early start, his growth continues. Glover is a graduate of New York University Tisch School of the Arts with a degree in Dramatic Writing. Prior to graduation, Glover was a disc jockey, producing music and writing for the sitcom *30 Rock*. His work in film and television, beginning in 1998, led to a starring role as Lando Calrissian in *Solo: A Star Wars Story* (2018) and his creation of the award-winning television series, *Atlanta*. Glover is a multi-award winner in music and film. No limit.
Award (select): Grammy Award (4 in 2019), Black Reel Award (2018, 2017), PGA Award (2018), Golden Globe (2017), Image Award (2017), Writers Guild of America (2017, 2010, 2009, 2008),

Critics Choice Television Award (2016), Primetime Emmy (2016), American Comedy Award (2012), TV Guide Award (2012)
Movie (producer and actor): *Guava Island* (2019)
Movie (actor): *The Lion King* (2019), *Solo: A Star Wars Story* (2018), *Spider-Man: Homecoming* (2017), *The Martian* (2015), *Magic Mike XXL* (2015), *The Lazarus Effect* (2015), *Alexander and the Terrible, Horrible, No Good, Very Bad Day* (2014), *Mystery Team* (2009)
Television Movie (actor): *Community: Abed's Master Key* (2012), *Winner Takes All* (1998)
Television (executive producer, writer, actor): *Atlanta* (2016-2018)
Television (executive story editor): *30 Rock (2008-2009)*
Television (actor): *Donald Glover Presents* (2019), *China, IL* (2015), *Community, (2009-2014), 30 Rock* (2006-2012), *UCB Comedy Originals* (2007-2010), *Bronx World Travelers* (2007)

Common aka Lonnie Rashid Lynn (1972), rapper, actor, executive producer, author, philanthropist. Expanding the scope of hip hop influence, Common won an Academy Award in 2015, along with John Legend, for Best Original Song, "Glory," for the movie *Selma*. He received an NAACP Image Award for acting in the film, as well. Recognized for consciousness-raising rap lyrics, his breakthrough mainstream album was "Like Water for Chocolate," in 2000. After several years of cameo and guest appearances in film and television, in 2006 Common attained a major acting role in the movie *Smokin' Aces* and has maintained a balanced career in music and film ever since. He seamlessly navigates between film and television, taking the lead in the 2006 movie *Just Wright,* with a major role in the television western *Hell on Wheels*. Starting with the movie *LUV* in 2012, Common fully developed his business sense for producing and executive producing a variety of well-received projects. He has authored several books that include *One Day It'll All Make Sense* and children's books *The Mirror and Me* and *I Like You, But I Love Me*. In 2007 Common started a full-service youth foundation, Common Ground Foundation, based in his birthplace Chicago, Illinois. Committed to health and fitness, Common created

a series called *Com+Well* on his YouTube channel in 2020.
Award: Grammy Award (2016, 2003), Academy Award (2015), BET Hip Hop Award (2014, 2007, 2006), Golden Globe (2015), Black Reel Award (2015), NAACP Image Award (2015)
Movie (producer, actor): *LUV* (2012)
Movie (executive producer): *Burning Sands* (2017)
Movie (actor): *Ava* (2020), *The Informer* (2019), *The Kitchen* (2019), *Run All Night* (2015), *Selma* (2014), *Every Secret Thing* (2014), *Now You See Me* (2013), *Movie 43* (2013), *The Odd Life of Timothy Green* (2012), *New Year's Eve* (2011), *Just Wright* (2010), *Date Night* (2010), *Wanted* (2008), *Street Kings* (2008), *American Gangster* (2007), *Smokin' Aces* (2006)
Documentary (executive producer): *40 Years a Prisoner* (2020), *They Fight* (2018), *America Divided* (2016), *Two Trains Runnin'* (2016), *Magic Men* (2013)
Television Movie (executive producer): *An American Girl: Melody 1963-Love Has to Win* (2016)
Television (executive producer, actor): *The Chi* (2018-2020, actor, 2018-2019), *Framework* (2015)
Television (actor): *The Lion Guard* (2017-2018, voice), *Hell on Wheels* (2011-14)

Da Brat aka Shawntae Harris (1974), rapper, actor, executive producer. Da Brat holds the distinction of being the first female solo rapper to go platinum in album sales in 1994 with her debut album, Funkdafied. Her talent radiates as the narrator for *Carmen: A Hip Hopera* in 2001 and *Civil Brand* in 2002. Da Brat ventured into her business side as an executive producer for the television series *Growing Up Hip Hop: Atlanta* (2017-2019). She has appeared in numerous reality television shows.
Award: Soul Train Lady of Soul Award (1995), Billboard Award (1995, 1994, two categories)
Movie: *30 Days* (2006), *Civil Brand* (2002), *Glitter* (2001), *Kazaam* (1996)
Television (executive producer, co-host): *Growing Up Hip Hop: Atlanta* (2017-2019)

David Banner aka Lavell William Crump (1974), rapper, actor, executive producer. David Banner brings scholastic achievement to hip hop. Born in Jackson, Mississippi, he graduated from Southern University with a BA in Business. By the time David Banner's highly praised rap recording *Get It Like Me* was being nominated for major awards, he had already gotten major film roles, starting in 2006 as Tehronne in the movie *Black Snake Moan*. Other lead roles were in *Lee Daniels' The Butler* in 2013 and *This Christmas* in 2007. In 2006 Banner was awarded the Visionary Award by the National Black Caucus of the State Legislature for his work after Hurricane Katrina. Several producing projects include the faith-based movie *Never Heard* (2016).
Movie (producer): *#DigitalLivesMatter* (2016)
Movie (producer, actor): *Never Heard* (2018)
Movie (actor): *The Last Punch* (2016), *Carter High* (2015), *Ride Along* (2014), *They Die by Dawn* (2013), *Lee Daniels' The Butler* (2013), *The Confidant* (2010), *Days of Wrath* (2008), *This Christmas* (2007), *Black Snake Moan* (2006)
Television Movie (executive producer, writer, actor): *That Crook'd Sip* (2007, voice)
Television Movie (actor): *Where's the Love* (2014), *A Christmas Blessing* (2013)
Television (actor): *Empire* (2019-2020), *Saints & Sinners* (2016-2017)

DJ Pooh aka Mark Jordan (1969), music and movie producer, rapper, screenwriter. Los Angeles, CA native, DJ Pooh produced his chart-topping *Bad Newz Travels* album, then continued to explore his creative expression. His influence as a record producer contributed to the early success of illustrious talents such as LL Cool J, The Dogg Pound, and 2Pac, to name a few. He wrote and directed the movies *The Wash*, released in 2001, and *3 Strikes*, released in 2000. Given his affinity for working behind the camera, DJ Pooh is also recognized for his writing and consulting for various *Grand Theft Auto* video game serials.
Movie (writer, producer, director, actor): *The Wash* (2001), *3

Strikes (2000)
Movie (writer, director): *Grow House* (2017)
Movie (writer and actor): *Friday* (1995)
Movie (writer): *Friday After Next* (2002), *Next Friday* (2000)
Movie (actor): *Trunkful* (2019)
Television (writer) *In the Flow with Affion Crockett* (2011)

DMX aka Earl Simmons (1970-2021), rapper, actor, executive producer. Born in Baltimore, Maryland, and raised in Yonkers, New York, DMX accomplished amazing feats early in his entertainment career. An underground sensation in the 1990s he is highly recognized for making history in 1998 by having two albums, *It's Dark and Hell Is Hot* and *Flesh of My Flesh, Blood of My Blood*, reach number one on the Billboard charts in the first week within the same year. 1998 also ushered in a fast-tracked promising career in cinema starting with *Belly*. By 2004 he assumed the role of producer and lead actor for *Never Die Alone*. In 2002 DMX was nominated for a Breakthrough Male Performance, MTV Movie Award for his 2001 role in *Exit Wounds*.
Award: BET Hip Hop Award (2006), Grammy (2001, 2000), Billboard Music Award (2001, 1999), American Music Award (2000), Soul Train Music Award (2000), The Source Award (1991)
Movie (executive producer and actor): *Last Hour* (2008), *Death Toll* (2008), *Jump Out Boys* (2008), *Never Die Alone* (2004)
Movie (actor, select): *Chronicle of a Serial Killer* (2020), *Beyond The Law* (2019), *The After Party* (2018), *Top Five* (2014), *The Bleeding* (2009), *Cradle 2 the Grave* (2003), *Exit Wounds* (2001), *Boricua's Bond* (2000), *Romeo Must Die* (2000), *Belly* (1998)
Television (producer, reality television): *DMX: Soul of a Man* (2006)

Doctor Dré aka Andre Brown (1963), veejay, deejay, rapper, actor, writer. Often complimented for his extremely upbeat attitude, Doctor Dré was one of the first effective advocates for recognizing hip hop and rap as legitimate music genres. Along with longtime business associate and entertainment partner Ed Lover, he pioneered the

role of veejay as a co-host of MTV's video music show *Yo! MTV Raps* from 1988 to 1995. Although much of Doctor Dré's career has been spent as a television and radio music host, there's been significant involvement with rap recordings and work in film and television. In 2018 he was honored by The 500 Men Making A Difference, Inc., based in New York City, for his contribution to music.
Movie (writer and actor): *Who's the Man?* (1993)
Movie (actor): *Fixing Rhonda* (2008), *Ride* (1998), *Juice* (1992)
Television (actor): *Miracle's Boys* (2005), *Yo! MTV Raps* (1988-1995, host)

Doug E. Fresh aka Douglas E. Davis (1966), rapper, beatboxer, actor, music, television executive producer. Born in Barbados and raised in New York, Doug E. Fresh, known as the original human beatbox, has sustained a viable diversified career. As a human beatbox, audiences marvel at his ability to use breath control, mouth, and throat as a musical instrument. After initial success, he teamed with rapper Slick Rick. After their hit singles "*The Show*" and "*La-Di-Da-Di*," Doug E.Fresh followed up with achievements as a music producer, television producer, and actor.
Award: BET Hip Hop Award (2014)
Movie (actor): *You're Nobody 'til Somebody Kills You* (2012), *Whiteboyz* (1999), *Let's Get Bizzee* (1993), *Tapeheads* (1988)
Television (executive producer and writer): *2013 Soul Train Awards* (2013)
Television Documentary (producer): *Hip Hop Cultural Odyssey: Know Your History* (2012)

Dr. Dre aka Andre Romelle Young (1965), executive producer, rapper, entrepreneur, actor. From club deejay to occupying a seat in the boardroom, Dr. Dre has achieved phenomenal success. He is recognized for the origin of West Coast G-Funk with hit singles and albums which include *The Chronic*, released in 1992. Born in Compton, California, Dr. Dre achieved primary entrepreneurial success as a music producer and founder of Beats Electronics. He's had stellar collaborations with Snoop Dogg and Eminem. Dr. Dre's first acting role in cinema was as Black Sam in *Set It Off* (1996). In 2001 he executive produced and acted in *The Wash*. He won the Maverick Movie Award in 2012 for best soundtrack for the documentary *Uprising: Hip Hop and the LA Riots*.

Award: Grammy Award (2020, 2010, 2001, 1994), BET Hip Hop Award (2015, 2014), Soul Train Music Award (2002, 2001, 1997), American Music Award (2001, 1994), MTV Video Music Award (2000, 1995), Billboard (1993)

Movie (producer) *Straight Outta Compton* (2015)

Movie (executive producer and actor): *The Wash* (2001)

Movie (actor): *Pauley Shore Is Dead* (2003), *The Wash* (2001), *Training Day* (2001), *Whiteboyz* (1999), *Set It Off* (1996)

Television Movie (actor): *Seriously…Phil Collins* (1990)

Drake aka Aubrey Drake Graham (1986), rapper, actor, executive producer. Fame runs high and intensity deep for the Toronto, Canada native. Drake was a television actor before rapping, starting in 2001. He established his acting career on the various *Degrassi* serial episodes, cast as Jimmy Brooks from 2001 to 2009. A descendent of a family of musicians, including his father and uncle, Drake always had his sight on music. His father, Dennis Graham is a professional drummer and his uncle, Larry Graham, was the founder of the band Graham Central Station and a band member with Sly and the Family Stone. His uncle, Teenie Hodges Graham was a guitarist and songwriter for Al Green. His mother, Sandra Graham is an educator. His innate talent and exposure have served him well. He has won countless awards throughout his music career. In 2012 and 2013 Drake took time to act in the movies *Ice Age: Continental Drift* and *Anchorman 2: The Legend Continues*. He returned to his television roots in 2019 as executive producer for the HBO television series *Euphoria*.

Award (select): BET Award (2020, 2019, 2018, 2016, 2015, 2014, 2013, 2012), Grammy Award (2020, 2019, 2017, 2013),

iHeartRadio Music Award (2020, 2017), Billboard Music Award (2019, 2017, 2015), iHeartRadio Music Award (2017), MTV Video Music Award, VMA (2016, 2014, 2012), Image Award (2012)
Movie (producer): *Spree* (2020)
Movie (actor): *Anchorman 2: The Legend Continues* (2013), *Ice Age: Continental Drift* (2012), *Charlie Bartlett* (2007)
Documentary (executive producer): *Ready for War* (2019), *The Carter Effect* (2017)
Television (executive producer): *Euphoria* (2019-2021),
Television Movie (actor): *Conviction* (2002)
Television (actor): *The Egos* (2018, season 3, episode 5, episode 20), *Degrassi: The Next Generation* (2001-2009), *Degrassi: Minis* (2005-2007), *Soul Food* (2002, season 2, episode 15), *Blue Murder* (2001)

Eminem aka Marshall Bruce Mathers III (1972), rapper, music producer, television executive producer, actor. Eminem has been given substantial credit for taking rap mainstream. He was born in St. Joseph, Missouri, and is of Scottish, Swiss, German, and English ancestry. A prolific writer, he musically composed his first major film project and won an Academy Award in 2003 for the best original song, *Lose Yourself,* featured in the 2002 movie release *8 Mile*. He also acted in the film. Eminem has written two autobiographies: *The Way I Am* (published, 2009) and *Angry Blonde* (published, 2002)
Award (select): MTV Europe Music Award (2017), Grammy Award (2015, 2011, 2010, 2004, 2003, 2001, 2000), People's Choice Award (2011), ASCAP Film and Television Music Award (2004), MTV Movie Award (2003), Teen Choice Award (2003)
Movie (producer): *Bodied* (2017)
Movie (actor and music composer): *8 Mile* (2002)
Movie (actor): *The Interview* (2014), *Funny People* (2009), *The Wash* (2001)
Television (executive producer): *Total Slaughter 1* (2015), *Eminem: Live from New York City* (2005)
Television (actor): *Entourage* (2010, season 7, episode 10)

Eve aka Eve Jihan Jeffers (1978), rapper, actor, executive producer. A Grammy Award and Teen Choice Award winner, Eve has collaborated with numerous rap and music icons. She was born in Philadelphia, Pennsylvania. Her transition to acting has been fluid, starting with the role of Teri, in the triumphant *Barbershop* franchise. Eve went on to executive produce and act in the highly-rated television comedy series, *Eve*.
Award: Grammy Award (2002), Washington DC Area Film Critics Association Award (2002), MTV Video Music Award (2001), NAACP Music Award (2000)
Movie (actor): *Jack Boyz* (2019), *Barbershop: The Next Cut* (2016), *Bounty Killer* (2013), *All Wifed Out* (2012), *Whip It* (2009), *Barbershop 2: Back in Business* (2004), *The Woodsman* (2004), *xXx* (2002), *Barbershop* (2002)
Television (executive producer and actor): *Eve* (2003-2006)
Television Movie (actor): *With This Ring* (2015)
Television (actor): *Feel Good* (2021), *Glee* (2009)

Fab 5 Freddy aka Frederick Brathwaite (1959), hip hop artist, actor, director, executive producer, television host. A former art student at Medgar Evers College, consummate hip hop artist Fab 5 Freddy is a noted painter and graffiti artist. Born in Brooklyn, New York, he has taken on numerous creative roles, including television cameraman. He also directed music videos in the late 1980s. His historic "Change the Beat" 12-inch single was recorded in both English and French. Fab 5 Freddy made history as the first hip hop veejay on the MTV show *Yo! MTV Raps,* from 1988 to 1995. He's made a variety of movie and television appearances, and associate produced the movie *New Jack City* in 1991. Additional contributions to hip hop culture are his involvement in consulting and producing hip hop honors award shows, primarily *VH1 Hip Hop Honors*. He was a *VH1 Hip Hop Honors* honoree in 2007 for his role in entertainment. In May 2019, The New York Public Library's Schomburg Center for Research in Black Culture in Harlem acquired the full archive of hip hop pioneer and pop culture icon Fab 5 Freddy.

Movie (producer, writer, director, composer): *Wild Style* (1983)
Movie (producer, actor): *New Jack City* (1991)
Movie (actor): *Barry* (2016), *Rachel Getting Married* (2008), *American Gangster* (2007), *The Manchurian Candidate* (2004), *She's Gotta Have It* (1986)
Documentary (director): *Grass is Greener* (2019)
Television (executive producer): VH1 Hip Hop Honors (2004-2009)
Television (actor, single episodes): *She's Gotta Have It* (2017, season 1, episode 6), *Blue Bloods* (2016, season 7, episode 4), *Luke Cage* (2016, season1, episode 13), *Law & Order: Criminal Intent* (2007, season 6, episode 14)

Fat Joe aka Joseph Antonio Cartagena (1970), rapper, actor, executive producer. Bronx, New York native, Fat Joe has always maintained a strong business ethic. From music to a retail owner to film, Fat Joe always has a sustainable project going on. He also practices community outreach, donating computers to high schools, and bringing attention to the danger of childhood obesity. He's amassed quite a few credits in movies and television, starting with the movie *I Like It Like That* in 1994. Movie and television projects have proved to be a staple.
Award: BET Hip Hop Award (2 in 2016, 2008), Soul Train Music Award (2 in 2016), Billboard Latin Music Awards (2006), ASCAP Rhythm & Soul Music Award (2005)
Movie documentary (director, executive producer): *Big Pun: Still Not A Player* (2002)
Movie (actor): *Fearless* (2020, voice), *Night School* (2018), *Lady Rider* (2017), *Supermodel* (2015), *Narx* (2011), *Happy Feet* (2006), *Empire* (2002), *Prison Song* (2001), *Blazin'* (2001), *Thicker Than Water* (1999), *Whiteboyz* (1999), *I Like It Like That* (1994)
Television Movie (actor): *New York Undercover* (2019), *The Cookout 2* (2011)
Television (actor): *She's Gotta Have It* (2017)

The Fat Boys-**Buff Love** aka Darren Robinson (1967-1995), **Rock-Kool Ski** aka Damon Wimbley (1966), and **Prince Markie Dee** aka Mark Morales (1968), rappers and actors. The Fat Boys were introduced during the 1980s rap music scene. Buff Love was highly recognized for his skills as "The Human Beatbox." All three were born in New York. They made a few film and television appearances individually, yet stood out as a team. Their most memorable films were *Disorderlies* in 1987 and *Knights of the City* in 1986. At various stages of their careers each pursued solo music projects. *Krush Groove* was their cinematic debut in 1985. The Fat Boys were nominated for several awards between 1987 and 1989.
Movie (acting as a trio): *Disorderlies* (1987), *Knights of the City* (1986), *Krush Groove* (1985)
Movie (**Kool Rock Ski**, actor): *My Crackhead Uncle* (2011)
Television (acting as a trio): *Miami Vice* (1986, season 2, episode 16)

50 Cent aka Curtis James Jackson III (1975), rapper, executive producer, actor, director, entrepreneur, author. A renaissance man with a deep appreciation for the arts, 50 Cent, born in Queens, New York, embraced and exposed his street credibility. He has profited greatly by it. 50 Cent has continually sought out and made the most of environments and experiences that contribute to personal and professional growth. He was attracted to producing films before acting in his first film, *Get Rich or Die Tryin'*, in 2005. Numerous movies 50 Cent produced have been shot and released in foreign countries, starring 'A' list actors. His domestic television productions do quite well: *Life* (2020) and *Power* (2014-20), in which he also acts, are testaments. In 2015 he had the opportunity to appear in *Southpaw,* a story that takes place in the world of boxing, a sport in which 50 Cent has a long history and appreciation. As an entrepreneur, he is the founder of several companies that include vitamin water, video games, clothing, and audio ventures. Many of these endeavors belong to the 'G-Unit' brand. The books he has written in various genres include a fitness book entitled *Formula 50: A 6-Week Workout and Nutrition Plan That Will Transform Your*

Life. 50 Cent's music achievements are massive, as an artist and producer.

Award (select): Hollywood Walk of Fame (2020), NAACP Image Award (2020), Grammy Award (2010), BET Hip Hop Award (2008), American Music Award (2005, 2003), Billboard Music Award (2005, 2004, 2003), Vibe Award (2005, 2004, 2003), BET Award (2004, 2003), The Source Award (2003), Teen Choice Award (2001)

Movie (producer, writer, actor): *All Things Fall Apart* (2011), *Gun* (2010)

Movie (producer and actor): *The Frozen Ground* (2013), *Fire with Fire* (2012), *Freelancers* (2012), *Setup* (2011), *Caught in the Crossfire* (2010)

Movie (actor): *Southpaw* (2015), *Spy* (2015), *The Prince* (2014), *Las Vegas* (2013), *Escape Plan* (2013), *13* (2010), *Twelve* (2010), *Dead Man Running* (2009), *Righteous Kill* (2008), *Home of the Brave* (2006), *Vengeance* (2006), *Get Rich or Die Tryin'* (2005)

Television (executive producer, director, actor): *Power* (2014-20)

Television (executive producer and actor): *For Life* (2020-2021)

Television (executive producer): *Power Book II: Ghost* (2020-2021), *Power Confidential* (2019-2020), *Dream School* (2014)

Documentary (executive producer): *The Game: Documentary* (2005), *50 Cent: The New Breed* (2003)

Fredro Starr aka Fred Lee Scruggs, Jr. (1971), rapper, actor, producer, author. New York native, former Onyx rap group member, Fredro Starr doesn't wait for opportunities, he makes them happen. Give him a day on a film lot and by the end of the day, he will sell an idea, be considered for an acting role, or both. His first acting part was in the television movie *Strapped*, directed by Forest Whitaker, released in 1993. By 1995 he was cast in Spike Lee's *Clockers* and the horror movie *The Addiction*. The recurring role of Quinton 'Q' Brooks on the hit television show *Moesha* solidified Fredro Starr as a recognized actor. He has also taken a departure from his hard-core rap beginnings to write two children's books, *Lil Freddy: The Red Sock,* in 2011, and *Lil Freddy: The Bully Kid*. With the group Onyx, he won the Soul Train Music Award in 1994

for Best Rap Album.
Award: Soul Train Music Award (1994)
Movie (producer, actor): *The Next Hit* (2008)
Movie (actor, select): *Equal Standard* (2020), *Duke* (2019), *The Fearless One* (2017), *Deceitful* (2013), *After Hours: The Movie* (2011), *Queen of Media* (2011), *Deceptz* (2011), *The Eddie Black Story* (2009), *Busted* (2009), *A Day in the Life* (2009), *My Brother* (2006), *Torque* (2004), *Save the Last Dance* (2001), *Light It Up* (1999), *Ride* (1998), *Sunset Park* (1996), *Clockers* (1995), *The Addiction* (1995)
Television Movie (actor): *Strapped* (1993)
Television (actor, select): *The Wire* (2001-2003), *Moesha* (1996-2000)

Fresh Prince aka Will Smith (1968), actor, comedian, executive producer, rapper, songwriter. One of the first commercially successful rappers to never have to resort to a curse word to enhance his verse, Will Smith, by appearance, effortlessly transitioned to cinematic blockbuster superstar. Endowed with qualities required of leading men; great look, charisma, Smith backs it up with extraordinary talent and drive. Making an auspicious movie debut in the teen drama *Where the Day Takes You* in 1992, Smith, as MC Fresh Prince with DJ Jazzy Jeff, had already carved out a celebrated career as the rapper half of the hip hop duo. A few movies and years later, the Philadelphia, Pennsylvania native became a household name as a star of the television hit *The Fresh Prince of Bel-Air*, which ran from 1990-96. He also performed and wrote the series theme song with Jazzy Jeff. Together, they won the first Grammy in the Rap category in 1989 for *Parents Just Don't Understand.* No stranger to starring in huge popular franchises such as *Bad Boys* and *Men in Black,* he also stellar performed biological portrayals in *Concussion* in 2015, *The Pursuit of Happyness* in 2006, and *Ali* in 2001. A savvy businessman, Smith prospers as a television and movie executive producer. He's worked in front and behind the camera with all of his nuclear family members: wife, actor, and executive producer Jada Pinkett Smith and children Trey, Jaden, and Willow. An abundant award winner, Smith is also recognized for his generous philanthropy.

Award (select): People's Choice Award (2020, 2009, 2005), All Def Movie Award (2016), MTV Movie Awards (2016, 2008, 2002, 1998, 1997), Palm Springs International Film Festival (2016), African American Film Critics Award (2015), Hollywood Film Award (2015), BET (2009, 2002), Kids' Choice Awards, USA (2009, 2006, 2005, 2003, 2000, 1998, 1991), NAACP Image Award (2009, 1999), Teen Choice Award (2008, 2007, 2005), American Music Award (2005), Blockbuster Entertainment Awards (1999, 1998, 1997), Grammy Awards (1999, 1998, 1992, 1988)

Movie (producer, writer, actor): *After Earth* (2013)

Movie: (executive producer, producer, select): *Life in a Year* (2020, executive producer), *Sprinter* (2018, executive producer), *Annie* (2014), *This Means War* (2012), *The Karate Kid* (2010), *The Secret Life of Bees* (2008), *ATL* (2006), *Saving Face* (2004), *The Seat Filler* (2004)

Movie (producer, actor): *Bad Boys for Life* (2020), *Seven Pounds* (2008), *Hancock* (2008), *The Pursuit of Happyness* (2006), *Hitch* (2005), *I Robot* (2004, executive producer)

Movie Documentary (executive producer): *Free Angela and All Political Prisoners* (2012)

Movie (actor, select): *Spies in Disguise* (2019, voice), *Gemini Man* (2019), *Aladdin* (2019), *Bright* (2017), *Collateral Beauty* (2016), *Suicide Squad* (2016), *Concussion* (2015), *Focus* (2015), *Men in Black 3* (2012), *I Am Legend* (2007), *Shark Tale* (2004), *Bad Boys II* (2003), *Ali* (2001), *The Legend of Bagger Vance* (2000), *Wild Wild West* (1999), *Enemy of the State* (1998), *Men In Black* (1997), *Independence Day* (1996), *Bad Boys* (1995), *Six Degrees of Separation* (1993), *Made In America* (1993), *Where the Day Takes You* (1991)

Television (executive producer): *Cobra Kai* (2021-2018), *All of Us* (2003-07), *The Fresh Prince of Bel-Air* (1995-96)

Television Documentary (executive producer): *Will Smith's Bucket List* (2019)

Television (actor): *All of Us* (2003-04), *Fresh Prince of Bel-Air* (1990-96), *ABC Afterschool Specials: Hawker* (1990)

The Game aka Jayceon Taylor (1979), rapper, actor, executive producer. A gentle giant by appearance, five gunshot wounds ushered The Game into the rap world. The captivating hip hop artist was born in Compton, California. His role as "Meat" in the 2006 movie *Waist Deep* earned him film acting credibility. He produced the highly-rated documentary *Game: Life After the Math*. The Game has also appeared and starred in several television reality shows, including *Change of Heart* (2000), *Marrying the Game* (2012-14), and *She's Got Game* (2015). Nominated for a Grammy Award in 2006, The Game has collaborated with major players in the music industry. Committed to functional training, conventional bodybuilding, and nutrition, he founded 60 Days of Fitness.
Award (all listed received in 2005): Billboard R&B/Hip-Hop Award, Justo Mixtape Award, Vibe Award, World Music Award
Documentary (executive producer): *Game: Life After the Math* (2008)
Movie (actor): *House Arrest* (2012), *Street Kings* (2008), *Tournament of Dreams* (2007), *Waist Deep* (2006)

Ice Cube aka O'shea Jackson (1969), rapper, actor, executive producer, writer, director. Undisputed, Ice Cube is a power player at the top of the entertainment game. Music, cinema, television; he's all in. Before initially pioneering West Coast gangsta rap with NWA, the Los Angeleno and dedicated family man made sure to safeguard his future by studying architectural drafting at the Phoenix Institute of Technology. Cast in the lead role of Doughboy in the 1991 film *Boyz n the Hood*, Ice Cube utilized a multitude of cinematic skills to solidify his career in film and television. Gaining a lead role in one's first film is rare. As a producer, he has a keen sense of what attracts an audience, offering diverse genres, be it biographical such as *Straight Outta Compton* (2015) or the family-friendly film, *Are We There Yet?* (2005) and as a television series (2010-12). The fact that Ice Cube is ceaselessly involved in a project, be it a movie or television acting, producing, writing, directing, or music, is testimony to a creative drive that's boundless.
Award (select): Hollywood Walk of Fame (2017), All Def Movie

Award (2017, 2016), AFI Movie Award (2016), Image Award (2011), BET Hip Hop Award (2009), Soul Train Music Award (2005), Urbanworld Film Festival Award (2005 and 2002), Blockbuster Entertainment (2000), Chicago Film Critics Association Award (1992).
Movie (executive producer, writer, director, music composer, actor): *The Players Club* (1998)
Movie (executive producer, producer, writer, actor): *The Janky Promoters* (2009), *All About the Benjamins* (2002), *Next Friday* (2000), *Friday* (1995, executive producer)
Movie (executive producer, producer, actor): *Fist Fight* (2017, executive producer), *Barbershop: The Next Cut* (2016), *Ride Along 2* (2016), *Ride Along* (2014), *Lottery Ticket* (2010, executive producer), *The Longshots* (2008), *First Sunday* (2008), *Are We Done Yet?* (2007), *Are We There Yet?* (2005), *Barbershop 2: Back in Business* (2004, executive producer), *Friday After Next* (2002), *Dangerous Ground* (1997, executive producer)
Movie (executive producer): *Beauty Shop* (2005)
Movie (producer): *Straight Outta Compton* (2015)
Movie (actor): *The High Note* (2020)
Television (executive producer): *Are We There Yet?* (2010-2012), *Black, White* (2006)
Television Documentary (executive producer): *P.O.V: Sierra Leone's Refugee All Stars* (2007)

Ice-T aka Tracy Lauren Marrow (1958), rapper, actor, executive producer, author. Original hard-core gangsta rapper, Ice-T is about impenetrable stability. Born in Newark, New Jersey, raised in Los Angeles, he works all angles; from heavy metal and bass rap beats to career sustaining two-decade role of Detective Odafin Tutuola on *Law & Order: Special Victims Unit* (2000-2021). The Grammy and NAACP Image Award winner presents a diversified acting range, starting with his breakout movie, *New Jack City* (1991). Ice-T attracts solid projects. His influence is apparent. Such is the case for the television series *In Ice Cold Blood* (2018-2020), *Ice & Coco* (2015), *Ice Loves Coco* (2011-2013), and *Players* (1997-

1998). Exceedingly busy acting in movies in the 1990s, Ice-T's first acting role was in the television series *Fame* in 1983. Early in his film career, Ice-T immediately understood the advantage of being involved in the business of film producing and seized opportunities. He's authored books which include *Ice: A Memoir of Gangster Life and Redemption-from South Central to Hollywood* and fiction, *Kings of Vice*.

Award: DOC LA (2019), Image Award (2002 and 1996), Grammy Award (1991)

Movie (executive producer, actor): *Equal Standard* (2020), *Crossed the Line* (2014), *Up in Harlem* (2004, associate producer), *The Wrecking Crew* (2000), *Corrupt* (1999), *Stealth Fighter* (1999)

Movie Documentary (executive producer): *Something from Nothing: The Art of Rap* (2012), *25 to Life: Ice T Presents* (2008)

Movie (actor): *Clinton Road* (2019), *UglyDolls* (2019, voice), *Bloodrunners* (2017), *How We Met* (2016, narrator), *Tracks* (2005), *On the Edge* (2002), *Out Kold* (2001), *Guardian* (2001), *Kept* (2001), *'R Xmas* (2001), *3000 Miles to Graceland* (2001), *Luck of the Draw* (2000), *Frezno Smooth* (1999), *Mean Guns* (1997), *Below Utopia* (1997), *Johnny Mnemonic* (1995), *Tank Girl* (1995), *Surviving the Game* (1994), *Who's the Man* (1993), *Trespass* (1992), *Ricochet* (1991), *New Jack City* (1991), *Breakin' 2: Electric Boogaloo* (1984), *Breakin'* (1984)

Television (executive producer): *Framed by the Killer* (2021), *In Ice Cold Blood* (2018-2020), *Ice Loves Coco* (2011-13), *The Peacemaker* (2010)

Television Movie (executive producer): *Planet Rock: The Story of Hip-Hop and the Crack Generation* (2011)

Television (writer, actor): *Players* (1997-98)

Television Movie (actor): *The Magic 7* (2009), *Exiled* (1998)

Television (actor): *Law & Order: Special Victims Unit* (2000-2021)

Ja Rule aka Jeffrey Bruce Atkins (1976), rap, singer, actor, executive producer. Born in Hollis, Queens, NY, the grit-infused melodic voice rapper/singer had a heated run of film releases between 2000 and 2010. Ja Rule returned to acting on the big screen in *I'm in Love with a Church Girl* (2013). He's appeared regularly on reality/documentary television. In 2019 Ja Rule took on the role of television executive producer of the reality show *Growing Up Hip Hop: New York.*

Award: BET Award (2002), GQ Men of the Year Award (2002), MTV Award (2002, 1999), NAACP Image Award (2002), Teen Choice Award (2002), World Music Award (2002),

Movies (actor): *Reboot Camp* (2020), *I'm in Love with a Church Girl* (2013), *Once Upon a Time in Brooklyn* (2013), *Don't Fade Away* (2010), *Furnace* (2007), *Back in the Day* (2005), *Shall We Dance?* (2004), *The Cookout* (2004), *Scary Movie 3* (2003), *Pauly Shore Is Dead* (2003), *Half Past Dead* (2002), *The Fast and the Furious* (2001), *Turn It Up* (2000)

Television (executive producer): *Growing Up Hip Hop: New York* (2019)

Television (movie, actor): *The Cookout 2* (2011)

Jay-Z aka Shawn Corey Carter (1969), rapper, executive producer, entrepreneur, philanthropist, social activist. Jay-Z is a pioneer and frontrunner in taking rap culture to diverse unparalleled heights. Born in Brooklyn, NY, much can be learned about Jay-Z's path to mega-success in his memoir *Decoded*, published in 2010. As for cinema, although he has dabbled in acting, in *State Property* (2002), he hit his stride as a film and documentary producer. His social activist side is revealed in executive producing the television miniseries *Rest in Power: The Trayvon Martin Story* (2018) and *Time: The Kalief Browder Story* (2017). The activist also illuminates as executive producer for the documentary *Free Angela and All Political Prisoners* (2012). Unlimited creative film interest is demonstrated with mainstream produced projects such as *Annie* (2014), *Top Five* (2014), and *The Great Gatsby* (2013). In 2019 Jay-z was presented the NAACP Image Award–President's Award. The award recognizes special achievement and public service. His Roc Nation entertainment company entered into a partnership with Long Island University to start the Roc Nation School of Music, Sports & Entertainment in 2020. The undergraduate focus will be

on music, music technology, entrepreneurship, production, and sports management.
Award (select): BET Award (2019, 2017, 2014, 2013, 2010, 2009, 2001), NAACP President's Award (2019), Billboard Music Award (2019, 2018, 2001, 1999), GLAAD Media Award (with Beyoncé 2019), Grammy Award (2019, 2017, 2015, 2014, 2012, 2011, 2010, 2009, 2006, 2005, 2004, 1999), People's Choice Award, USA (2010), Soul Train Award (2007, 2001)
Movie (executive producer; producer): *Annie* (2014), *Top Five* (2014), *The Great Gatsby* (2013, executive producer), *Paid in Full* (2002)
Movie Documentary (executive producer): *Made in America* (2013), *Free Angela and All Political Prisoners* (2012), *Black Sorority Project: The Exodus* (2006), *Fade to Black* (2004)
Movie (actor): *State Property* (2002)
Television Documentary (executive producer): *Free Meek* (2019), *Rest in Power: The Trayvon Martin Story* (2018), *Time: The Kalief Browder Story* (2017), *Jay-Z in Concert* (2003)
Television (executive producer) *Noughts + Crosses* (2020)

Jim Jones aka Joseph Guillermo Jones II (1976), rapper, executive producer, actor, entrepreneur. There's no taking a break from business for Jim Jones, he's involved in sports management, fashion design, reality television, music video directing. Bring the right project to the table and he is there. Born in Bronx, New York, his music career started in 1997 with the Diplomats and took off in 2000. Soon after, acting followed, with appearances in *Paper Soldiers* (2002) and *State Property: Blood on the Streets* (2005). Jim Jones has done extremely well with reality television projects as an executive producer and cast member. His initial mainstream television introduction was on *Love & Hip Hop* (2011-2012). Jim Jones personifies stability in the rap profession, which can be attributed to his business acumen and loyalty to longtime collaborators. He's been nominated for the Soul Train Award and the Urban Music Award.
Documentary (executive producer): *Red Apples Falling* (2009),

This Is Jim Jones (2009), *Jim Jones: A Day in the Fast Lane* (2006, also the director)
Movie (actor): *All In* (2019), *First Lady* (2018), *Righteous Kill* (2008), *Who's Deal?* (2008), *State Property: Blood on the Streets* (2005), *Paper Soldiers* (2002)
Television (executive producer and cast member): *Chrissy & Mr. Jones* (2012)
Television (actor): *The Wire* (2008, season 5, episode 8)

Kid 'n Play aka Christopher Reid (**Kid**, 1964), rapper, actor. Christopher Martin (**Play**, 1962), rapper, actor. Both were born in New York; Kid in the Bronx, and Play in Queens. As a team, they represented a fun-loving, family-friendly side of rap. They pioneered acting in the quintessential hip hop movies, starting with *House Party* in 1990. Success soared as they appeared together, between 1990 and 1994, in House *Party 2* (1991), *Class Act* (1992), and *House Party 3* (1994). After an amicable split, they both continue to pursue acting and producing.
Movie, Kid (producer, video): *Sword of Honor* (1996)
Movie, Kid (actor): *Pauly Shore Is Dead* (2003), *House Party 3* (1994), *Class Act* (1992), *House Party 2* (1991), *House Party* (1990)
Television Movie, Kid (actor): *Funny Business* (2014), *Freaknik: The Musical* (2010), *Bodyguards* (1993)
Television, Kid (actor): *Black Dynamite* (2012-2014), *Barbershop* (2005), *The Temptations* (1998), *Sister, Sister* (1996-1997), *Minor Adjustments* (1996), *Kid 'n Play* (1990)
Movie, Play (actor): *Movie Madness* (2016), *Rising to the Top* (1999), *House Party 3* (1994), *Class Act* (1992), *House Party 2* (1991), *House Party* (1990)
Television Movie, Play (actor): *Funny Business* (2014), *Bodyguards* (1993)
Television, Play (executive producer): *Fail* (2012)
Television, Play (actor): *Church Folks* (2020), *Kid 'n Play* (1990)

Lauryn Hill (1975), rapper, singer, writer, actor, executive producer. Born in Newark, New Jersey, Lauryn Hill was recognized as an actor before her breakthrough as a music artist. Success with the Fugees eventually led to a lucrative solo music career. In the early 90s, Lauryn Hill first appeared on television in a recurring role as teen Kira Johnson in *As the World Turns*. By 1993, with the release of *Sister Act 2: Back in the Habit,* Lauryn Hill had to decide between pursuing acting, music, or continuing her first year at Columbia University. She chose to focus on music. In 2020 she produced the award-winning *Why Is We Americans?,* a documentary that examines the legacy of social activism by writer Amiri Baraka and his family.
Award (select): Grammy Award (2000, 1999, 1997), Soul Train Award (2000, 1999), American Music Award (2000, 1999), NAACP Image Award (1999), Billboard Music Award (1998), Brit Award (1997), World Music Award (1997), MTV Video Music Award (1996)
Documentary (executive producer): *Why Is We Americans?* (2020), *Mic Check Live: Ms. Lauryn Hill & Tyrese Gibson* (2011)
Movie (actor): *Restaurant* (1998), *Hav Plenty* (1997), *Sister Act 2: Back in the Habit* (1993), *King of the Hill* (1993)
Television (actor): *ABC Afterschool Special: Daddy's Girl* (1996), *As the World Turns* (1991)

Lil' Bow Wow aka Bow Wow aka Shad Gregory Moss (1987), rapper, actor, executive producer. Bow Wow has been in entertainment for the majority of his life. Born in Columbus, Ohio, Bow Wow started as a professional rapper at age six. After a few turns at acting in 2001 on television's *Moesha* and the television movie *Carmen: A Hip Hopera,* he was ready to lead in the movie *Like Mike* in 2002. By the time he hosted BET'S *106 & Park Top 10 Live* and appeared in the movie *Lottery Ticket* in 2010, his career in film and television was secure.
Award: Billboard Music Award (2001), Kid's Choice Award (2001), BET Award (2001)
Movie (actor): *Furious 7* (2015), *Scary Movie 5* (2013), *Allegiance* (2012), *Madea's Big Happy Family* (2011), *Lottery Ticket* (2010),

Hurricane Season (2009), *Roll Bounce,* (2005), *Johnson Family Vacation* (2004), *Like Mike* (2002)
Television (executive producer): *Growing Up Hip Hop: Atlanta* (2017-2020)
Television Movie (actor): *In Broad Daylight* (2019), *Saving Jason* (2003), *Smart and Sober* (2003), *Carmen: A Hip Hopera* (2001)
Television (actor): *The Masked Singer* (2020), *CSI: Cyber* (2015), *106 & Park Top 10 Live* (2000-14) *Entourage* (2008-09)

Lil' Kim aka Kimberly Denise Jones (circa the mid-1970s), rapper, actor, writer, executive producer. The key to Lil' Kim's success is her ability to remain fluid. From being a sensuous entertainer to an actor to a savvy businesswoman, she's turned adversity into an advantage. Such was the case when she executive produced *Lil Kim: Countdown to Lockdown* (2006), for television. The Bedford-Stuyvesant, Brooklyn, New York native reigns in front and behind the scene. Her big-screen acting skills were utilized in *She's All That* (1999). Since then, Lil' Kim has appeared in film and television, including reality television. Early in her rap career, she had what it took to be signed to the prestigious Wilhelmina Model Agency to endorse high-end designer products. "Queen Bee" uses her celebrity to raise awareness of social causes; AIDS research, in particular. Lil' Kim applies her writing skills to the majority of her music videos.
Award: BET Award (2019), Grammy Award (2002), MTV Video Music Award (2002, 2001, 1998), Teen Choice Award (2001)
Movie (actor): *Superhero Movie* (2008), *Nora's Hair Salon* (2004), *You Got Served* (2004), *Gang of Roses* (2003), *Juwanna Mann* (2002), *Zoolander* (2001), *She's All That* (1999)
Television (executive producer): *Girls Cruise* (2019), *Lil' Kim: Countdown to Lockdown* (2006)
Television (actor): Single appearances in numerous episodic television series throughout the years, starting in 1999.
Television (reality and variety): *RapFix Live* (2011-2013), *Dancing With The Stars* (2009), *Entertainment Tonight* (2009), *Pussycat Dolls Present: Girlicious* (2008)

Lil' Romeo aka Romeo aka Percy Romeo Miller (1989), rapper, actor, executive producer. Born in New Orleans, Louisiana, Romeo had the advantage of being Master P's son. His talent solidifies his position. It takes skill to deliver rhymes for most seasoned adults, let alone a child. By the time he was eleven, he showcased his acting talent on the Nickelodeon Television Network's, *The Brother's Garcia* (2001). A role in *Max Keeble's Big Move* (2001) followed. Romeo formerly attended the University of Southern California as a basketball player and a business major. Romeo's film and television career thrived with his television series, *Romeo!* (2003-2006). He executive produced the television series *Growing Up Hip Hop* (2016-2020).
Award: Kid's Choice Award (2005), Radio Disney Music Award (2003), Billboard Music Award (2001)
Movie (executive producer): *Never and Again* (2021)
Movie (select, actor): *I Got the Hook Up 2* (2019), *Game Day* (2019), *Never Heard* (2018), *Destruction Los Angeles* (2017), *A Girl Like Grace* (2015), *Brotherly Love* (2015), *Frat Brothers* (2013), *Madea's Witness Protection* (2012), *Jumping the Broom* (2011), *Down and Distance* (2010), *Uncle P* (2007)
Television (executive Producer): *Master P Reviews* (2021), *No Limit Chronicles* (2020), *Growing Up Hip Hop* (2016-2020)
Television (actor) *The Brothers Garcia* (2001, season 2, episode 5)

Lil Wayne aka Dwayne Michael Carter, Jr. (1982), rapper, executive producer, actor. Lil Wayne wrote raps before age ten and joined Cash Money Records by age 12. He was an honor student in high school when he dropped out at age 14 to pursue his music career. During his music career, he earned his GED and attended the University of Houston and University of Phoenix, a psychology major. His writing skills are also apparent in his memoir *Gone 'Til November: A Journal of Rikers Island,* published in 2016. New Orleans, Louisiana-born, Lil Wayne never shied away from substantial speaking parts, starting with the role of Iceberg Shorty in *Baller Blockin* (2000). He co-starred with Birdman aka Bryan Christopher Williams. Nine years later, there was a major role in

the movie *Hurricane Season,* followed by a succession of television acting and executive producing projects. Lil Wayne is very involved in charitable causes, especially in his hometown of New Orleans.
Award (select): American Music Award (2017), BET Award (2017, 2015, 2011, 2010, 2009, 2008, 2007), Grammy Award (2017, 2009), Billboard Music Award (2012), Soul Train Award (2011), MTV Video Music Award (2008)
Movie (actor): *Hurricane Season* (2009), *Baller Blockin'* (2000)
Television (documentary, executive producer): *Nicki Minaj: My Time Now* (2010), *Drake: Better Than Good Enough* (2010)
Television Movie (actor): *Freaknik: The Musical* (2010), *Blueprint: Lil Wayne* (2008)
Television (series appearances, actor): *The Masked Singer* (2020, season 3, episode 1), *The Boondocks* (2007), *The Roaches* (2006)

L.L. Cool J aka James Todd Smith (1968), rapper, actor, producer. The first rapper to be recognized by Kennedy Center Honors, L.L. Cool J was born in Bay Shore, Long Island, New York. As a boy, he knew he wanted to rap and was signed to the Def Jam label by the time he was a teenager. While still in his teens he appeared in the movie *Wildcats* (1986). As an actor, his career took off in the film *The Hard Way* (1991). L.L. Cool J's music and film success have culminated in superior achievement in both categories. Aside from being television host extraordinaire of the *Grammy Awards* and *Lip Sync Battle,* he capped his interest in entrepreneurial endeavors by completing the Business of Entertainment Media & Sports program at Harvard University. He's authored and co-authored numerous books, particularly on the subject of fitness, and has written an autobiography with Karen Hunter titled *I Make My Own Rules.*
Award: NAACP Image Award (2018, 2014, 2013, 2012, 2011), Kennedy Center Honors (2017), Walk of Fame (2016), Teen Choice Award (2013), BET Comedy Award (2004), ShoWest Convention, USA (2003), Blockbuster Entertainment Award (2000), Grammy (1997, 1992), MTV Video Music Award (1997, 1991), Soul Train Award (1987)

Movie (actor): *Grudge Match* (2013), *The Deal* (2008), *Last Holiday* (2006), *Slow Burn* (2005), *Edison* (2005), *Mindhunters* (2004), *S.W.A.T.* (2003), *Deliver Us from Eva* (2003, *Kingdom Come* (2001), *Charlie's Angels* (2000), *Any Given Sunday* (1999), *In Too Deep* (1999), *Deep Blue Sea* (1999), *Halloween H20: 20 Years Later* (1998), *Woo* (1998), *Caught Up* (1998), *B*A*P*S* (1997), *Out-of-Sync* (1995), *Toys* (1992), *The Hard Way* (1991), *Wildcats* (1986)
Television movie (producer, actor): *The Man* (2007)
Television (producer, host): *Lip Sync Battle* (2015-2019), *The Grammy Nominations Concert Live!: Countdown to Music's Biggest Night* (2009)
Television (actor): *NCIS: Los Angeles* (2009-2021), *In the House* (1995-1999)

Ed Lover aka James Roberts (1963), rapper, actor, executive producer, director, writer, television and radio host. Mass media personality, Ed Lover holds the distinction of being the star along with Doctor Dré aka Andre Brown, in his second film, *Who's the Man?* (1993). He and Doctor Dré also wrote the story, which was adapted for the screen by Seth Greenland. *Who's the Man* featured appearances by a cavalcade of rap artists such as Ice-T, Fab 5 Freddy, and Salt–N-Pepa. During the late 1980s to mid-1990s, Ed Lover and Doctor Dré hosted *Yo! MTV Raps*. Born in Hollis Queens, New York, Ed Lover makes television appearances as an actor while maintaining a lucrative radio host career.
Movie (writer, actor): *Who's the Man?* (1993)
Movies (actor): *Come Sunday* (2018), *Undisputed* (2002), *Ride* (1998), *Juice* (1992)
Television (executive producer, director): *The '90's: We Invented This* (2015)
Television (host): *Yo! MTV Raps* (1988-1993)

Ludacris aka Christopher Brian Bridges (1977), rapper, actor, executive producer, record executive. Champaign, Illinois native with an exuberant voice, Ludacris began his entertainment career as a deejay. One of the first southern rappers to go mainstream, his film career has profited greatly with his starring in *The Fast and the Furious* movie franchise. From 2003 to 2021, Ludacris has appeared as the character Tej Parker. The former Georgia State University music management major is also recognized for his dramatic roles in *Hustle & Flow* (2005) and *Crash* (2004). As a television host and guest, Ludacris is well received. He has won his share of music and acting awards. An entrepreneur and philanthropist, he's involved with the Do Something campaign, Better World Books, and The Ludacris Foundation.

Award: CMT Music Award (2018), MTV Video Music Award (2010, 2005, 2004), BET Award (2007, 2004), Grammy Award (2007, 2005), Broadcast Film Critics Association Award (2006), Screen Actors Guild (2006), Billboard Music Award (2005, 2004), Hollywood Film Award (2005), Teen Choice Award (2005)

Movie (executive producer, actor): *John Henry* (2020), *The Ride* (2018)

Movie (actor): *F 9* (2021), *Show Dogs* (2018), *The Fate of the Furious* (2017), *Furious 7* (2015), *Fast & Furious 6* (2013), *New Year's Eve* (2011), *Fast Five* (2011), *No Strings Attached* (2011), *Gamer* (2009), *Max Payne* (2008), *RocknRolla* (2008), *Ball Don't Lie* (2008), *Fred Claus* (2007), *Hustle & Flow* (2005), *Crash* (2004), *2 Fast & 2 Furious* (2003), *The Wash* (2001)

Television (documentary, executive producer): *ATL: The Untold Story of Atlanta's Rise in the Rap Game* (2014)

Television Movie (actor, narrator): *Jim Henson's Turkey Hollow* (2015)

Television (appearances, actor): *Empire* (2015), *Being Mary Jane* (2014), *Eve* (2005)

Marky Mark aka Mark Wahlberg (1971), rapper, model, actor, executive producer. Success for the rap group *Marky Mark and the Funky Bunch* was fast. Their short span as a rap group led to tremendous opportunities. Born in Boston, Massachusetts, Marky Mark's tough, racist history has been well documented. Disciplinary measures and an abundance of positive exposure brought about a change in racial outlook. His extremely lucrative modeling and endorsement career led to film stardom. Initially, he was credited as Marky Mark for guest spots on scripted television shows. When his first major movie role in the film *Renaissance Man* (1994) debuted, his screen name changed to his given name, Mark Wahlberg. His choice for movie and television producing projects is impressive, starting with *Juvies* (2004). He executive produced and narrated *Juvies*, which was co-narrated by Mos Def (Yasiin Bey). Twice nominated for an Academy Award for acting in *The Fighter* (2010) and *The Departed* (2006), Marky Mark has made the utmost of opportunities afforded him. Having dropped out of school at a very early age, he returned in his forties and earned his high school diploma for himself and set an example of completion for his children. For his extensive contribution to charitable causes, he was presented with the Humanitarian Award in 2021.

Award (select): Humanitarian Award (2021), Realscreen Award (2019), Critics Choice Movie Award (2014, 2011), MTV Movie+TV Award (2014) African-American Film Critics Association Award (2010), Boston Society of Film Critics Award (2010), Hollywood Walk of Fame (2010), Blockbuster Entertainment Award (2000)

Movie (producer): *Stealing Cars* (2015), *Entourage* (2015), *Prisoners* (2013)

Movie (producer and actor): *Spenser Confidential* (2020), *Instant Family* (2018), *Mile 22* (2018), *Daddy's Home Two* (2017), *Patriots Day* (2016), *Deepwater Horizon* (2016), *Entourage* (2015), *The Gambler* (2015), *Lone Survivor* (2013), *Broken City* (2013), *Contraband* (2012), *The Fighter* (2010), *Juvies* (documentary, 2004)

Movie (actor, select): *Joe Bell* (2020), *Scoob!* (2020), *All the Money in the World* (2017), *Transformers: The Last Knight* (2017), *Daddy's Home* (2015), *Ted 2* (2015), *Transformers: Age of Extinction* (2014), *2 Guns* (2013), *Pain & Gain* (2013), *Ted* (2012), *The Other Guys* (2010), *Date Night* (2010), *The Lovely Bones* (2009), *We Own the Night* (2007), *Shooter* (2007), *The Departed* (2006), *Invincible* (2006), *Four Brothers* (2005), *I Heart Huckabees* (2004), *The Italian Job* (2003), *Rock Star* (2001), *Planet of the Apes* (2001),

The Perfect Storm (2000), *The Yards* (2000), *Three Kings* (1999), *The Corrupter* (1999), *The Big Hit* (1998), *Boogie Nights* (1997), *Traveller* (1997), *Fear* (1996), *The Basketball Diaries* (1995), *Renaissance Man* (1994)
Television Documentary (executive producer): *McMillions* (2020)
Television Movie (executive producer): *The Missionary* (2013), *Home Game* (2011)
Television (executive producer): *In Treatment* (2008-2021), *The Lost Lincoln* (2020), *Run This City* (2020), *Ballers* (2015-2019), *Shooter* (2016-2018), *Boardwalk Empire* (2010-2014), *Wahlburgers* (2014), *Teamsters* (2013), *Entourage* (co-producer and actor, 2004-2011*), How to Make It in America* (2010-2011)
Television Movie (actor): *The Substitute* (1993)
Television Appearances (actor): *Out All Night* (1993), *The Ben Stiller Show* (1993)
Television (reality): *Wahlburgers* (2014-2019)

Master P aka Percy Robert Miller (1970), rapper, entrepreneur, executive producer, actor, athlete, philanthropist. At his core, Master P is all about business and being the optimal humanitarian. His primary focus is youth and seniors. He calls attention to mental illness being overlooked in the African American community. There was a No Limit record shop before there was a No Limit record label. Born in New Orleans, Louisiana, his scope is broad. Master P is a firm outspoken believer in 'ownership'. Every endeavor he gets involved in, he sets out to own, or brand; be it a record label, retail product, property, stocks, or media. Master P was one of the first rappers to understand and implement how to transform the art of rap into a mega-money-making enterprise. Raised in an impoverished environment and unable to find work at a very young age, he realized he would have to create a way for himself. He started by selling cell phones. For a short time, he attended the University of Houston on a basketball scholarship. From there he enrolled in courses in business management at Merritt College; a community college in Oakland, California. With a ten thousand dollar inheritance from the passing of his grandfather, he was able to purchase his first business, a record store in Richmond, California. Then he got his music up and going, started a label, moved back to Louisiana, and grew his empire. In true Master P style, immediately after his first movie acting role in *The Players Club* (1998), he wrote, acted, and executive produced *I Got The Hook Up* (1998). Aside from executive producing and acting, he took a turn directing the movie *No Tomorrow* (1999). Having made many guest appearances on television, he has lucratively produced shows, such as *Romeo!* (2003-2006), the reality television shows *Growing Up Hip Hop* (2016-2020) and *Master P's Family Empire* (2015-2016). His book, *Guaranteed Success: When You Never Give Up,* was released in 2017 by Percy "Master P" Miller. Renowned for promoting self-determination, ownership, and giving back to the community, a percentage of the sales from every one of his Moneyatti luxury sneakers sold goes to social causes. Inner-city communities with educational resources and programs in place to help build futures are a primary focus.

Award: BET Hip Hop Award: I Am Hip-Hop Icon Award (2020), Louisiana Music Hall of Fame (2013), Acapulco Film Festival (2000), American Music Award (1999)

Movie (writer, producer, actor): *I Got the Hook Up 2* (2019), *The Mail Man* (2009), *Uncle P* (2007), *Foolish* (1999), *I Got the Hook Up* (1998)

Movie (executive producer, director, actor): *No Tomorrow* (1999)

Movie (executive producer, actor): *Never and Again* (2020), *Lockdown* (2000)

Movies (actor): *Never Heard* (2018), *Destruction Los Angeles* (2017), *Killing Hasselhoff* (2017), *Down and Distance* (2010), *The Pig People* (2009), *Soccer Mom* (2008), *Toxic* (2008), *Paroled* (2007), *Dark Blue* (2002), *Undisputed* (2002), *Takedown* (2000), *The Players Club* (1998)

Documentary (producer) *Desert Bayou* (2007)

Television (creator, executive producer, actor): *Romeo!* (2003-2006)

Television (executive producer): *Growing Up Hip Hop* (2016-2020), *No Limit Chronicles* (2020), *Master P's Family Empire* (2015-2016)

Television (actor): *Moesha* (2000)

MC Hammer aka Stanley Kirk Burrell (1961), rapper, dancer, choreographer, actor, executive producer, entrepreneur, minister. Speaking of "no curse in the verse," you'd be hard-pressed to hear it in Oakland, California native MC Hammer's raps. He raps great gospel, as well. His rich career history is anything but a straight line. As a boy, he was honorary Vice President for the Oakland A's baseball team. Time in college and honorary discharge from the U.S. Navy are backgrounds for his complex, colorful life. An entrepreneur who paved the way for rapper commercial endorsements, MC Hammer produced and starred in *Please Hammer, Don't Hurt 'Em* (1990), for which he earned a Grammy Award. In 1991 he followed up as the voice of the superhero cartoon character Hammerman for the television series *Hammerman*. MC Hammer is responsible for countless firsts, including being one of the first rap artists to integrate the television music video format. With a reputation as a rescuer, this is exactly what he did when called upon by film director Justin Lin to contribute producing funds to complete the making of *Better Luck Tomorrow*, released in 2002.
Award (select): George and Ira Gershwin Award (Lifetime Musical Achievement, 2013), American Music Award (1992, 1991, 1990), Soul Train Award (1992, 1991), Grammy Award (1991, multiple), Brit Award (1991), People's Choice Award (1991), Billboard (1990)
Movie (actor): *Zoolander 2* (2016), *Finishing the Game* (2007), *Deadly Rhapsody* (2001), *Private Parts* (1997), *Cheyenne* (1996), *Reggie's Prayer* (1996), *One Tough Bastard* (1996), *Last Action Hero* (1993)
Television (executive producer, reality television) *Hammertime* (2009)
Television Movie (actor) *The Right Connections* (1997)
Television (actor) *Hammerman* (1991, voice)

MC Lyte aka Lana Michelle Moorer (1970), rapper, actor, television host, producer, philanthropist. The possibility for rappers and hip hop artists, female and male, to be active in other media platforms is fueled by the trailblazing talent of MC Lyte. Born in Brooklyn, New York, the record sales-breaking rap artist has developed auspicious prospects when presented. The distinctive voice of the former Hunter College attendee can be recognized narrating numerous award shows presented on BET and VH1. Her visibility is high as a host on network television and as a voiceover for product endorsements. Appearing in recurring roles on several episodic television series, MC Lyte's first movie role was in *Fly By Night* (1992). Her prominence grew with the television comedy series *Half & Half* (2004-2006). In the role of mentor, MC Lyte has authored faith-based motivational books. As a businesswoman, she is recognized for her philanthropy and for her leadership roles, which include being past President, Trustee and Governor of the Los Angeles Chapter of the Recording Academy (Grammy Organization).

Award: Trumpet Award (2019), BET Lifetime Achievement Award (2013), VH1 Hip Hop Honors (2006), Soul Train Award (1996)

Books: *Living In the Lyte: Lessons in Life, Love and Truth* (2014), *Unstoppable: Igniting the Power Within to Achieve Your Greatest Potential* (2012)

Movie (actor): *Angie: Lost Girls* (2020), *Sylvie's Love* (2020), *Bad Hair* (2020), *Loved To Death* (2019), *Girl's Trip* (2017), *Patti Cake$* (2017), *The Dempsey Sisters* (2013), *Playas Ball* (2003), *Civil Brand,* (2002), *Train Ride* (2000), *A Luv Tale* (1999), *Fly By Night* (1992)

Documentary (producer): *Be Inspired: The Life of Heavy D* (2012)

Television Movie (actor): *New York Undercover* (2019)

Television (actor): *Queen of the South* (2017-2018), *S.W.A.T.* (2018), *A Celebration of American Creativity: In Performance at the White House* (2016), *Half & Half* (2004-2006), *For Your Love* (1998-2002)

Method Man aka Clifford M. Smith Jr. (1971), rapper, actor, executive producer, writer. Method Man's career in acting is impressive. His range is from a comedian to fierce drama. Prior to acting, he rapped with the Wu-Tang Clan. Redman (Reginald Noble) is also a music and acting collaborator. Born in Hempstead, NY, Method Man has predominantly been featured in highly-rated film productions. Teamed musically with Mary J. Blige in 1996, they won a Grammy. In 1997, his auspicious acting debut was in the role of Dennis Broadway in the movie *One Eight Seven*. In 2004 Method Man and Redman were featured in the acclaimed television comedy series *Method & Red*. The movie *How High*, released in 2001, introduced them as an irreverent comedic duo. Method Man maintains his stature continuously acting in film and television projects such as *Shaft* (2019) and *Power Book II: Ghost* (2020-2021).

Award: NAACP Image Award (2021), Grammy (1996)

Movie (actor): *Vampires vs. the Bronx* (2020), *Concrete Cowboy* (2020), *Shaft* (2019), *Jay and Silent Bob Reboot* (2019), *Peppermint* (2018), *Future World* (2018), *Love Beats Rhymes* (2017), *Where's The Money* (2017), *Peterson* (2016), *Keanu* (2016), *Lucky Number* (2015), *The Cobbler* (2014), *Red Tails* (2012), *The Sitter* (2011), *The Mortician* (2011), *Saints and Sinners* (2010), *The Wackness* (2008), *The Heart Specialist* (2006), *Venom* (2006), *Soul Plane* (2004), *Garden State* (2004), *How High* (2001), *Hwasango* (2001, English version), *Boricua's Bond* (2000), *Belly* (1998), *Cop Land* (1997), *One Eight Seven* (1997)

Television Movie (actor): *The Breaks* (2016), *Seasons of Love* (2014)

Television (executive producer): *Wu-Tang: An American Saga* (2019)

Television (executive producer and actor): *Method & Red* (2004)

Television (actor): *Power Book II: Ghost* (2020-2021), *Teenage Bounty Hunters* (2020), *The Last O.G.* (2019-2020), *The Deuce* (2017-2019), *Rebel* (2017), *The Breaks* (2017), *Blue Bloods* (2015-2017), *Chozen* (2014), *CSI: Crime Scene Investigation* (2006-2010), *The Wire* (2003-2008), *Oz* (2001)

Mos Def aka Yasiin Bey (1973), rapper, actor, executive producer. Yasiin Bey (as he prefers to be acknowledged) has experienced a fluid career in the entertainment industry. His early introduction to acting in plays, film, and television hit a high note before success in music. His caliber of acting is notable. The social activist was born in Brooklyn, New York. In 2002 he and actor Jeffrey Wright won the Outer Critics Circle Award for their joint performance in the Suzan-Lori Parks' Pulitzer Prize-winning play *Topdog/Underdog.* His film career launched with a co-starring role in the television movie *God Bless the Child* (1988). An early movie casting was *The Hard Way* (1991). Yasiin Bey donned a producer's hat as executive producer/host of the television series *Def Poetry* (2002-2007).

Awards: MuchMusic Award (2017), Black Reel Award (2008 and 2005), NAMIC Vision Award (2005), Obie Award (2003), Outer Critics Circle Special Award (2002)

Movies (actor): *Tour de France* (2016), *Life of Crime* (2013), *Begin Again* (2013), *I'm Still Here* (2010), *Next Day Air* (2009), *Cadillac Records* (2008), *Be Kind Rewind* (2008), *Talladega Nights: The Ballad of Ricky Bobby* (2006), *Journey to the End of the Night* (2006), *16 blocks* (2006), *The Hitchhiker's Guide to the Galaxy* (2005), *The Woodsman* (2004), *The Italian Job* (2003), *Brown Sugar* (2002), *Civil Brand* (2002), *Showtime* (2002), *Monster's Ball* (2001), *Bamboozled* (2000), *Where's Marlowe?* (1998), *The Hard Way* (1991)

Television movies (actor): *Lackawanna Blues* (2005), *Something the Lord Made* (2004), *Carmen: A Hip Hopera* (2001), *The Cosby Mysteries* (1994), *God Bless the Child* (1988)

Television (executive producer and host): *Def Poetry* (2002-2007)

Television (actor): *Dexter* (2011), *The Boondocks* (2005-2008), *Chappelle's Show* (2003-2006), *NYPD Blue* (1997-2000), *The Cosby Mysteries* (1994-1995), *Here and Now* (1992), *You Take the Kids* (1990-1991)

Nas aka Nasir bin Olu Dara Jones (1973), rapper, writer, actor, executive producer, entrepreneur. Nas is as much about business as he is about being an artist. Born in Brooklyn, music is in his DNA; his father, Olu Dara is a jazz musician. He rose to fame as the result of a brilliant hip hop music career in the mid-1990s with the album *Illmatic,* which was inducted into the National Recording Registry in 2021. Nas's interest as a highly successful entrepreneur almost runs parallel to his music acclaim.

He first blazed onto the big screen as co-writer and actor in the movie *Belly* (1998). His producing choice, *Survival 1,* was awarded a Sports Emmy Award for outstanding sports documentary in 2011. Nas has a keen interest in producing thought-provoking documentaries. His creative prowess has earned him the honor of Harvard University's establishment of the Nasir Jones Hip Hop Fellowship.

Award: Grammy Award (2021), BET Hip Hop Award (2012, 2006), Sports Emmy Award (2011), Vibe Award (2004)

Movie (executive producer, writer, actor): *Sacred Is the Flesh* (2001)

Movie (executive producer, actor): *Monster* (2018)

Movie (writer, actor): *Belly* (1998)

Documentary (executive producer): *Smoke Marijuana + Black America* (2020), *Shake the Dust* (2014), *Tyson* (2008)

Movie (actor): *Popstar: Never Stop Never Stopping* (2016), *Black Nativity* (2013), *Uptown Girls* (2003), *John Q* (2002), *Ticker* (2001)

Television Documentary (producer, writer, director): *Survival 1* (2011)

Television (executive producer): *The Get Down* (2016), *The Land* (2016)

Television (actor): *Great Performances-Nas Live From the Kennedy Center: Classical Hip-Hop* (2018), *Hawaii Five-0* (2010)

Nicki Minaj aka Onika Tanya Maraj (1982), rapper, writer, actor, executive producer. Some performers must have a project going at all times. Nicki Minaj is one of them. It appears as if making a video is just another workout. Given all her video performances, it should come as no surprise that the multi-platinum recording artist set out early in her career to be an actor. Born in Saint James, Port of Spain, Trinidad and Tobago, Nicki Minaj is recognized for her laser-focused perfectionism. Her marked business side is evident in the plethora of products she endorses and has a stake in.

Her voiceover role in the full-length movie *Ice Age: Continental Drift* (2012) was Nicki Minaj's entrance into acting on the big screen. By 2016 she was taking on the character of Draya in *Barbershop: The*

Next Cut. For television, she executive produced the documentary *Nicki Minaj: My Truth* (2012).
Award (partial list): BET Award (2020, 2017, 2016, 2015, 2014, 2013, 2011, 2010), American Music Award (2020, 2015, 2012, 2011), MTV Video Music Award (2019, 2018, 2015, 2012, 2011), Peoples Choice Award (2018), Billboard (2013, 2012, 2011)
Movie (actor): *The Angry Birds Movie 2* (2019), *The Other Woman* (2014), *Ice Age: Continental Drift* (2012)
Television (executive producer): *Nicki Minaj: My Truth* (2012)
Television Movie (actor): *Dave Skylark's Very Special VMA Special* (2014)
Television (actor): *Steven Universe* (2014-2016)

Nipsey Hussle aka Ermias Joseph Asghedom (1985-2019), rapper, songwriter, entrepreneur, activist, actor. Mega-brilliant and on the threshold of following through on his huge potential is one way to describe Nipsey Hussle before his extinguished light. He was a hustler who made the most of his exposure as he grew into a man willing to take on great responsibility. Nipsey Hussle made a conscious effort to commit to positive growth and change for the sake of his family and community. The BET Humanitarian Award winner was born in Los Angeles, California. East African, Eritrean roots on his father's side, he celebrated his cultural identity. His entrepreneurial spirit led him to skip requisite steps. With his first mixtape, *Slauson Boy Volume 1,* when he wasn't handing tapes out free, for exposure, he was selling them for one hundred dollars apiece. He operated several businesses which were a boost for the Crenshaw community in Los Angeles, CA, while simultaneously elevating his music career. He took the opportunity to act in two movies: *Caged Animal* (2010) and *I Tried* (2007). He also made a television appearance on *Crazy Ex-Girlfriend* (2015). Nipsey Hussle was committed to high-quality artistry, establishing peace, and promoting the type of community growth that leads to independence.
Awards: BET (2020, 1 award, 2019, 3 awards), Grammy (2020, 2 awards)

Movies (actor): *Caged Animal* (2010), *I Tried* (2007)
Television Documentary (self): *The L.A. Marathon (2019)*
Television (actor): *Crazy Ex-Girlfriend* (2015, season1, episode1)

Pras Michel aka Prakazrel Samuel Michel (1972), rapper, executive producer, actor. New York native, Pras Michel's creative talent was initially recognized as a member of the musically eclectic hip hop group, Fugees. Once the Fugees went separate ways, he achieved notoriety as a solo music artist; most notably with *Ghetto Supastar* (1998). Not resting on laurels of music success, Pras Michel ventured into acting, his first film being *Mystery Men* in 1999. He immediately applied his proclivity for producing to the movie *Turn It Up* in 2000. In 2015 and 2016 he produced in several different mediums: television, cinematic movie, and documentary. Acknowledged as a social activist, Pras Michel produced the documentaries *Sweet Mickey for President* (2015) and *Skid Row* (2007). Health-conscious, he doesn't smoke anything or indulges in drinking alcohol. Pras Michel received an Honorary Award at the Haiti Movie Awards in 2015.
Award (select): Grammy Award (1997), Brit Award (1997), World Music Award (1997), MTV Video Music Award (1996)
Movie (producer, actor): *Mutant Chronicles* (2008), *Go for Broke* (2002), *Higher Ed* (2001, executive producer), *Turn It Up* (2000)
Movie (producer): *Miles Ahead* (2015)
Movie (actor): *Feel the Noise* (2007), *Go Go Tales* (2007), *Nora's Hair Salon* (2004), *Mystery Men* (1999)
Documentary (producer): *Sweet Mickey for President* (2015, also a writer), *Skid Row* (2007, also acted)
Television (producer): *The Bay* (2015-2016)
Television (actor): *Fastlane* (2002)

Puff Daddy aka P. Diddy aka Sean John Combs (1969), rapper, executive producer, actor, entrepreneur, philanthropist, humanitarian. From contributing to education to being politically responsible, Sean Combs gives generously to the cause he promotes. He had a variety of businesses up and going while attending Howard University as a business major. Working as an intern at Uptown Records, the seeds of his music career were planted. Success in entertainment was imminent. Born in New York, steadfast and constant, Sean Combs has constructed a multi-mega conglomerate. He absorbed the best of environments his career path exposed him to, enhancing and enriching his existence. As a driving force in the music industry, he guided such acts as Notorious B.I.G and Mary J. Blige. He is invested in visual arts. Aside from film, television, acting, and producing, Sean Combs makes bold commentary via his streaming television network, Revolt TV. He is a huge proponent that the right to vote be exercised. A versatile actor, he has an endearing comic side while possessing intensity for drama. In 2009 he won the NAACP Image Award for Outstanding Actor in the role of Walter Lee Younger in the television movie *A Raisin in the Sun*. The highly acclaimed movie *Dope* was one of his film endeavors as executive producer in 2015. Sean Combs has a large stake in producing reality television, starting with *Run's House* (2005-2009). A founder of charter schools and a philanthropist, he was honored at the 2020 Grammy Salute To Industry Icons in recognition of his 25-year career and "continuous influence on the music industry and beyond."

Award (select): Hermes Creative Award (2018), Hollywood Film Award (2017), The BET Honors Entrepreneur Award (2010), People's Choice Award (2010), NAACP Image Award (2009), Hollywood Walk of Fame (2008), Soul Train Music Award (2003, 1998), Grammy Award (1998), World Music Award (1998, multiple), MTV Video Music Award (1998, 1997), Billboard Music Award (1997, multiple)

Movie (executive producer): *Dope* (2015), *Notorious* (2009)

Movie (actor): *Girls Trip* (2017), *Draft Day* (2014), *I'm Still Here* (2010), *Get Him to the Greek* (2010), *Carlito's Way: Rise to Power* (2005), *Monster's Ball* (2001), *Made* (2001)

Documentary (executive producer): *Anatomy of Black Art* (2020), *Anatomy of Black Love* (2020), *Can't Stop, Won't Stop: A Bad Boy Story* (2017), *Undefeated* (2011), *Nicki Minaj: My Time* (2010), *If I Were King: Sean John Internship by Design* (2008), *The Bad Boys*

of Comedy (2005 and 2007)
Television Movie (executive producer, actor): *A Raisin in the Sun* (2008)
Television (executive producer, writer): *Run's House* (2005-2009)
Television (executive producer, select): *State of the Culture* (2018-2019), *Icon Award Gala Honoring Queen Latifah* (2017), *Revolt Sessions* (2016), *Revolt 2 Vote Presents* (multiple episodes in 2016), *Mic Check Live: Ms. Lauryn Hill & Tyrese Gibson* (2011), *Daddy's Girls* (2009), *Taquita & Kaui* (2007), Making *the Band* (series 2,3 and 4 from 2002-2007)
Television Documentary (director) *Diddy Runs the City* (2003)
Television (actor): Single appearances in numerous episodic television series, starting in 2002

Q-Tip aka Jonathan Davis (1970), rapper, executive producer, actor, philosopher. Scholarly, when interviewed on the status of the music industry. For New York native Q-Tip, success with the hip hop alternative jazz-rap group A Tribe Called Quest preceded his going solo musically. The award-winning group consisted of Q-Tip, Phife Dawg, Ali Shaheed Muhammad, and Jarobi White. His first major screen performance was in the role of Markell in *Poetic Justice* (1993). He wrote, produced, and acted in the triumphant movie musical *Prison Song,* released in 2001. *The Hip Hop Project* was a documentary he produced in 2006. In 2016 Q-Tip was appointed to serve as Artistic Director on the Kennedy Center Hip Hop Culture Council. Never abandoning music and open to film, in 2018 Q-Tip elected to teach at New York University.
Award: Brit Award (2017), Grammy Award (2006), Billboard R&B/Hip-Hop Award (2005), The Source Award (1994)
Movie (writer, executive producer, actor): *Prison Song* (2001)
Movie (actor): *Holy Rollers* (2010), *Cadillac Records* (2008), *She Hate Me* (2004), *Love Goggles* (1999, narrator), *Poetic Justice* (1993)
Documentary (producer) *The Hip Hop Project* (2006)
Television Movie (actor) *Disappearing Acts* (2000)
Television (actor): *Happily Ever After: Fairy Tales for Every Child*

(2000, season 3, episode 11)

Queen Latifah aka Dana Owens (1970), rapper, songwriter, actor, talk show host, executive producer, entrepreneur, philanthropist. Queen Latifah is an entrepreneurial whirlwind. She unleashed her awe-inspiring business skills immediately after the success of her first album *All Hail the Queen* (1989), investing in a video store and delicatessen. By 1991 she was Chief Executive Officer of Flavor Unit Records and Management Company. By 1995 it had spawned into Flavor Unit Entertainment. Founded with Shakim Compere, Flavor Unit Entertainment is a production powerhouse in the film, television, and home entertainment industry. After several years of appearing as an actor in film and television, her initial venture into producing was her television talk show, *The Queen Latifah Show* (1999). She is the first hip hop artist to receive a star on the Hollywood Walk of Fame (2006) and the first female rapper to be nominated for an Academy Award. Queen Latifah is a contributor to numerous organizations dedicated to health initiatives, building self-esteem and diversity in music, film, and television. A multiple award winner, two socially conscious television movie triumphs were the NAACP Image Award for *Flint* (2018) and the Golden Globe Award for *Life Support* (2008).
Award (select): NAACP Image Award (2018, 2016, 2008, 2004,), Screen Actors Guild Award (2016, 2008, 2003), Primetime Emmy Award (2015), The BET Honors Media Award (2010), Critic's Choice Movie Award (2008, 2003), Golden Globe Award (2008), Kid's Choice Awards, USA (2007,2005), Glamour Award for The Role Models (2006), BET Award (2003), Black Reel Award (2003), Teen Choice Award (2003), Grammy Award (1995), Soul Train Music Award (1995)
Movie (executive producer): *The Secrets of Emily Blair* (2016), *The Perfect Match* (2016), *Brotherly Love* (2015), *November Rule* (2015), *Percentage* (2014), *Who's Your Caddy?* (2007), *House Party 2* (1991)
Movie (producer): *I Kissed a Girl* (2012), *The Cookout* (2005)
Movie (executive producer, actor): *The Trap* (2019), *House of*

Bodies (2013), *Joyful Noise* (2012), *Bringing Down the House* (2003)
Movie (producer, actor): *Just Wright* (2010), *The Perfect Holiday* (2007), *Beauty Shop* (2005)
Movie (actor, select): *Girls Trip* (2017), *Ice Age: Collision Course* (2016, voice), *Miracles From Heaven* (2016), *Ice Age: Continental Drift* (2012, voice), *The Secret Life of Bees* (2008), *Hairspray* (2007), *Ice Age: The Meltdown* (2006, voice), *Last Holiday* (2006), *Chicago* (2002), *Brown Sugar* (2002), *Living Out Loud* (1998), *Hoodlum* (1997), *Set It Off* (1996), *Juice* 1992, *House Party 2* (1991), *Jungle Fever* (1991)
Documentary (executive producer): *Ballet After Dark* (2019), *The Art of Organized Noize* (2016)
Television Movie (executive producer): *The Clark Sisters: First Ladies of Gospel* (2020), *The Real MVP: The Wanda Durant Story* (2016), *Let the Church Say Amen* (2013), *The Cookout 2* (2011), *Wifey* (2007)
Television Movie (producer): *Salt-N-Peppa* (2021)
Television Movie (executive producer, actor): *Flint* (2017), *Bessie* (2015), *Steel Magnolias* (2012), *Life Support* (2007)
Television (executive producer): *Scream: The TV Series* (2019), *The Rap Game* 2016-2019, *The Pop Game* (2017), *Curvy Style with Timothy Snell* (2016), *From the Bottom Up* (2016), *Let's Stay Together* (2011-2014), *The Next* (2012)
Television (executive producer, actor): *The Equalizer* (2021), *Star* (2018-2019, producer), *The Queen Latifah Show* (host, 2013-2014), *Single Ladies* (2011-2012), *The Queen Latifah Show* (host, 1999-2001)
Television (producer, actor): *Star* (2018-2019)
Television (actor, select): *Hollywood* (2020), *When the Streetlights Go On* (2020), *Living Single* (1993-1998)

RZA aka Robert Fitzgerald Diggs (1969), rapper, executive producer, actor, director. Co-founder and member of Wu-Tang Clan, RZA is a native of Brooklyn, NY. He suitably applied his disciplined music industry skills to filmmaking, music scores, producing, writing, acting, and directing. RZA was the driving force and executive producer of the award-winning eleven-episode biography drama *Wu-Tang: An American Saga*. He wrote and directed the martial arts film *The Man with the Iron Fists,* starring Russell Crowe and Lucy Liu (2012). In 2003 RZA worked with Quentin Tarantino to score the music for *Kill Bill: Volume 1.* As an actor, he's taken on substantial roles in film and television, which include the television series *Gang Related* (2014) and *Californication* (2012). A martial arts enthusiast, RZA applies the skill in his artistry.

Award: St. Louis Film Critics Association (2012), Central Ohio Film Critics Association (2004), Echo Award (2004), Source Award (1994)

Movie (producer, director): *Cut Throat City* (2020)

Movie (executive producer): *Meet the Blacks* (2016)

Movie (executive producer, actor): *Thriller* (2018)

Movie (writer, director): *The Man with the Iron Fists* (2012)

Movie (director): *Love Beats Rhymes* (2017)

Movie (actor, select): *Life in a Year* (2020), *The Dead Don't Die* (2019), *Popstar: Never Stop Never Stopping* (2016), *Mr. Right* (2015), *Brick Mansions* (2014), *The Protector 2* (2013), *G.I. Joe: Retaliation* (2013), *A Very Harold & Kumar Christmas* (2011), *The Next Three Days* (2010), *Repo Men* (2010), *Funny People* (2009), *Life Is Hot in Cracktown* (2009), *Gospel Hill* (2008), *American Gangster* (2007), *The Box* (2007), *Derailed* (2005), *Be Cool* (2005), *Coffee and Cigarettes* (2003)

Documentary (executive producer): *Dirty: One Word Can Change the World* (2009)

Television movie (actor): *Afro Samurai: Resurrection* (2009)

Television (executive producer, writer): *Wu-Tang: An American Saga* (2019)

Television (actor): *Gang Related* (2014), *Californication* (2012)

Snoop Dogg aka Calvin Cordozar Broadus Jr. (1971), rapper, executive producer, actor, entrepreneur. Snoop Dogg's early will and determination led to life-changing success. A persona that is cool and deliberate has matured to project a sage-like quality.

From his first number one selling rap album *Doggystyle* to movies, television, and a plethora of endorsements, Snoop Dogg's career has continually remained relevant. He has withstood the test of time. The Long Beach, California native has been true to giving back to his community and other philanthropic endeavors which include the Snoop Youth Football League and providing essentials to those at risk in Los Angeles County. His development is boundless; rap, write, act, and executive produce. The commercial television success *Martha & Snoop's Potluck Party Challenge* is one among many producing projects. Acting roles have contributed greatly to Snoop Dogg's notoriety, starting with his first cinematic character in *Half Baked* (1998). He won an MTV Movie Award for the role of Blue in *Training Day* (2002). His executive-produced documentary *Uprising: Hip Hop and the LA Riots* won the Beverly Hills Film Festival Award and the Maverick Movie Award in 2012. In 2018 Snoop Dogg switched gears and produced an award-winning gospel album, *Bible of Love*.

Award (select): BET Award (2019, 2016, 2003), The Streamy Award (2019), Hollywood Walk of Fame (2018), Independent Music Award (2018), MTV Video Music Award (2015, 2006, 1994), YouTube Music Award (2015), Beverly Hills Film Festival (2012), Maverick Movie Award (2012), MTV Movie Award (2002), Billboard Music Award (2001, 1994), Soul Train Music Award (1995)

A Selection of Snoop Dogg Producing Projects:

Movie (executive producer, actor): *Unbelievable !!!!!* (2020), *Meet the Blacks* (2016), *Mac & Devin Go to High School* (2012), *Down for Life* (2009)

Documentary (executive producer): *Coach Snoop* (2016), *Take Me to the River* (2014), *Uprising: Hip Hop and the LA Riots* (2012)

Television (executive producer, host, actor): *Go Big Show* (2021, judge), *GGN: Snoop Dogg's Double G News Network* (2011-2020), *Doggy Fizzle Television* (2002-2003)

Movie (actor, select): *The SpongeBob Movie: Sponge on the Run* (2020, voice), *The Addams Family* (2019, voice), *Dolemite Is My Name* (2019), *Trouble* (2019, voice), *Popstar: Never Stop Never Stopping* (2016), *Turbo* (2013, voice), *Falling Up* (2009), *The Tenants* (2005), *Racing Stripes* (2005, voice), *Soul Plane* (2004),

Starsky & Hutch (2004), *Bones* (2001), *Training Day* (2001), *Baby Boy* (2001), *Caught Up* (1998), *Half Baked* (1998)
Television (actor, select): *Utopia Falls* (2020, voice)
Stageplay (actor): *Redemption Of A Dogg* (2018)

T.I. aka Clifford Joseph Harris Jr. (1980), rapper, singer, executive producer, actor, writer, political activist, entrepreneur. T.I. is passionate and outspoken about the status of humanity as a whole, including reparation. Charitable works and activism don't interfere with his artistry. Born in Atlanta, Georgia, T.I.'s music career received a tremendous boost in 2004. In 2006 he auspiciously entered the world of cinema in the role of Rashad in *ATL*. Television has welcomed his father figure role in the reality show *T.I. & Tiny: The Family Hustle,* which also stars his wife, Tomeka (Tiny) Harris. In 2017 T.I. was nominated by Black Reel Awards for Outstanding Supporting Actor in his role as Cyrus in the 2016 television release of *Roots*. In 2020 he took a lead role in the RZA-directed *Cut Throat City*. T.I. has attracted a solid fan base for novels he wrote with David Ritz: *Trouble & Triumph: A Novel of Power & Beauty* (2012) and *Power & Beauty: A Love Story of Life on the Streets* (2011). For television, in support of up and coming hip-hop music talent, he executive produced the NAACP Image Award-winning *Rhythm + Flow*.
Award (select): Outer Critics Circle Award (2018), Billboard Music Award (2014, 2006), Soul Train Award (2013), BET Award (multiple categories, 2009, 2007, 2006), American Music Award (2007), Grammy Award (2007)
Movie (producer, actor): *Takers* (2010)
Movie (actor, select): *Monster Hunter* (2020), *Cut Throat City* (2020), *Dolemite Is My Name* (2019), *Ant-Man and the Wasp* (2018), *Krystal* (2017), *Sleepless* (2017), *Popstar: Never Stop Never Stopping* (2016), *Ant-Man* (2015), *Entourage* (2015), *Get Hard* (2015), *American Gangster* (2007), *ATL* (2006)
Television (executive producer): *Rhythm + Flow* (2019), *The Grand Hustle* (2018), *Sisterhood of Hip Hop* (2014), *T.I.'s Road to Redemption* (2009)

Television (actor, select): *Genius: Aretha* (2021), *The Breaks* (2017), *Roots* (2016), *T.I. & Tiny: The Family Hustle* (reality tv, 2015-2017), *Single Ladies* (2012-2014), *House of Lies* (2014), *Boss* (2012)

Treach aka Anthony Criss (1971), rapper, actor, producer. Treach's involvement in acting came rather quickly on the heels of his rap music success with the group Naughty By Nature. Recognized for his fit physique, the East Orange, New Jersey native earned his first credited speaking role in the 1993 movie *Meteor Man* after a walk-on part in the film *Juice* (1992). Treach has kept occupied as a television actor, with roles in television movies and appearances on various episodic series. Before taking on the role of producer for the movie *Equal Standard*, released in 2020, Treach co-produced the 2016 Realscreen Award-winning documentary *Black Market with Michael K. Williams*.
Award (with Naughty By Nature): Grammy Award (1996), American Music Award (1992)
Movie (producer, actor): *Equal Standard* (2020)
Movie (actor, select): *Six 2 Six* (2017), *One Blood* (2012), *Zoo* (2012), *A Day in the life* (2009), *Playas Ball* (2007), *Feast* (2005), *Love and a Bullet* (2002), *Book of Love: The Definitive Reason Why Men Are Dogs* (2002), *Empire* (2002), *Face* (2002), *3 A.M.* (2001), *Jason's Lyric* (1994), *The Meteor* (1993), *Juice* (1992)
Television Documentary (producer): *Black Market with Michael K. Williams* (2016)
Television Movie (actor): *The Verdict* (2008), *13 Graves* (2006), *Conviction* (2002), *Baseball Wives* (2002), *Rhapsody* (2000), *First Time Felon* (1997)
Television (actor): *Blue Bloods* (2017, season 8, episode 8), *The Night Of* (2016, season 1, episodes 5 and 6)

Tupac aka 2PAC aka Tupac Amaru Shakur (1971-1996), rapper, actor, activist. Tupac excelled tremendously during his brief life span. *All Eyez on Me* and his *Greatest Hits* collection are certified diamond, top-selling albums of all time. His single, *Changes,* was entered on the Vatican official playlist. Tupac's first cinematic appearance was with his fellow Digital Underground music group members in the movie *Nothing But Trouble* (1991). He was born in New York, NY, and primarily raised in the San Francisco Bay Area. After his role as Bishop in *Juice* (1992), his leading man opportunities took off at phenomenal speed. In *Poetic Justice* (1993) Tupac demonstrates his range as an actor. There was a television appearance on an episode of *A Different World* in 1993. Recognition for Tupac's artistry earned induction into the Rock and Roll Hall of Fame (2017) and the Library of Congress National Recording Registry (2010).

Award: Rock and Roll Hall of Fame (2017), ASCAP Rhythm & Soul Music Award (2005), American Music Award (1997), Soul Train Music Award (1996, 1997), MOBO Award (1996)

Movie (actor): *Gang Related* (1997), *Gridlock'd* (1997), *Bullet* (1996), *Poetic Justice* (1993), *Juice* (1992), *Nothing But Trouble* (1991, appearance with group Digital Underground)

Television (actor): *A Different World* (1993, season 6, episode 21), *Drexell's Class* (1992, season1, episode 17*)*

Wyclef Jean aka (select) Nel Ust Wyclef Jean (1969), rapper, writer, political activist, actor, executive producer. According to former Fugees rap group member Wyclef Jean: "Hip-Hop didn't have to be about thug life. It could just be about life." Born in Croix-des-Bouquets, Haiti, and raised in New Jersey, the artist carried his political activism as far as to run for president of Haiti in 2010. He was ruled ineligible due to a residency requirement. Wyclef Jean took on the role of Richie in the 2002 movie *Shottas* after making his first television appearance as an actor in the television movie *Carmen: A Hip Hopera* (2001). In 2005 he was nominated for a Golden Globe Award for co-writing the song *Million Voices* for the movie *Hotel Rwanda.* His acting skills were utilized in the highly-rated television series *Nashville* (2012-2013) and *Third Watch* (2005). Wyclef Jean showcased his talent as an author in 2012 when he co-wrote his biography, *Purpose: An Immigrant's Story* with author Anthony Bozza. For his vast charitable efforts, Wyclef Jean has received numerous humanitarian awards and recognition, including the President of Haiti, Michel Martelly, awarding him the National Order of Honour and Merit. He received the Black Entertainment Television Humanitarian Award in 2009 and was inducted into the New Jersey Hall of Fame in 2017.

Award: Cinemoi CinéFashion Film Award (2018), YouTube Creator Award (2017), NAACP Image Award (2010), BET Award (2009), Satellite Award (2005), Grammy Award (2000, 1997), MTV Award (1998)

Movie (actor): *Black November* (2012), *Dirty* (2005), *One Last Thing* (2005), *Be Cool* (2005), *Shottas* (2002)

Documentary (executive producer): *Ghosts of Cite' Soleil* (2006)

Television Movie (writer, actor): *Wyclef Jean in America* (2006)

Television (actor): *Law & Order: Special Victims Unit* (2016, season 18, episode 6), *Nashville* (2012-2013), *Third Watch* (2005), *Carmen: A Hip Hopera* (2001)

Xzibit aka Alvin Nathaniel Joiner (1974), rapper, actor, writer, executive producer. The affable Xzibit became a household name as host and consulting producer of the reality television show *Pimp My Ride* from 2004 to 2007. Born in Detroit, Michigan, the multi-platinum recording artist initially gained popularity with the *At the Speed of Life* album. Television has been a staple for Xzibit, as evidenced in his recurring role on the hit show *Empire* (2016-2019). Roles in critically acclaimed movies such as *American Violet* (2008) have also showcased his acting skills. For the television mini-series *Broken Ground* (2019-2020), he took his turn at writing and directing, as well as acting. Xzibit is a firm believer in lifting others to elevate yourself.

Movie (actor, select): *Bad Lieutenant: Port of Call New Orleans* (2009), *American Violet* (2008), *Gridiron Gang* (2006), *Hoodwinked* (2005), *Derailed* 2005), *xXx: State of the Union* (2005), *8 Mile* (2002), *The Wash* (2001), *The Breaks* (1999)

Documentary (executive producer, director) *Xzibit: Restless Xposed* (2001)

Television (writer, director, actor): *Broken Ground* (2019)
Television Movie (actor): *Seal Team Six: The Raid on Osama Bin Laden* (2012), *Weekends at Bellevue* (2011)
Television (actor): *Empire* (2016-2019), *Hawaii Five-0* (2013-2015), *Extreme Makeover: Home Edition* (2009-2012), *Gumball 3000 med Erik och Mackan* (2010), *Pimp My Ride* (2004-2009)

Yo-Yo aka Yolanda Whitaker (1971), rapper, actor, educator. Having evolved into the role of hip hop mentor, Yo-Yo remains increasingly relevant; a pioneer specifically representing west coast female rappers. Born in Compton, California, a protégé of Ice Cube, Yo-Yo has been exposed to and worked with the best in the music industry. In 1996, she was nominated for a Grammy Award for vocal performance on *Stomp,* in collaboration with Quincy Jones. Before that, she was nominated for an MTV Music Award in collaboration for *I Wanna Be Down* featuring Brandy, MC Lyte, and Queen Latifah. They reunited for a stellar performance on *VH1Hip Hop Honors: All Hail the Queens* in 2016. Yo-Yo brought a positive energy with her television presence on *Love & Hip Hop: Hollywood.* Her initial casting was in the classic *Boyz n the Hood,* released in 1991, followed by *Menace II Society* in 1993. Yo-Yo has appeared in numerous movie and television roles, including the television series *Martin*. She took time out to attend Bergen Community College in New Jersey and earn an associate degree. Yo-Yo founded The School of Hip Hop summer programs in Los Angeles for youth, to not only increase their skill at rhymes and beats; they're also taught how to get A's in English through hip hop. According to Yo-Yo: "I don't teach them how to write rhymes; I teach them how to write."
Movie (actor): *Janitors* (2016), *Waist Deep* (2006, Female Radio DJ voice), *The Breaks* (1999), *Sprung* (1997), *Panther* (1995), *Sister Act 2: Back in the Habit* (1993), *Menace II Society* (1993), *Who's the Man?* (1993), *Boyz n the Hood* (1991)
Television Movie (actor): *Trails of Life* (1997), *Strapped* (1993)
Television (actor, select): *Unsolved: The Murders of Tupac and the Notorious B.I.G.* (season 1, episode1, 2018), *Martin* (1993-1995)

Television (self, reality): *Love and Hip Hop: Hollywood* (2019), *Miss Rap Supreme* (2008, host)

RAP TO CINEMA HONORABLE MENTION

John Singleton (1968-2019)

The Notorious B.I.G. aka Christopher George Latore Wallace (1972-1997)

Beanie Sigel aka Dwight Equan Grant

Birdman aka Bryan Christopher Williams

Bun B aka Bernard James Freeman

Cardi B aka Belcalis Marlenis Almánzar

Damon Dash

DJ Khaled aka Khaled Mohamed Khaled

Big Sean aka Sean Michael-Leonard Anderson

Foxy Brown aka Inga DeCarlo Fung Marchand

Jermaine Dupri aka Jermaine Dupri Mauldin

Juelz Santana aka LaRon Louis James

Mack 10 aka Dedrick D'mon Rolison

Missy Elliott aka Melissa Arnette Elliott

Mystikal aka Michael Lawrence Tyler

Rah Digga aka Rashia Fisher

Wiz Khalifa aka Cameron Jibril Thomaz

Kanye West

Honorable Mention (Continued From)
Third Edition: Ready For Your Close Up?
African Americans And Internationals In Cinema Who Are College Graduates

by G. Shields

James Edwards (1918-1970) actor, screenwriter, MA in Drama, Northwestern University

Thomas Jefferson Byrd (1950-2020), actor, producer

Kathleen Collins (1942-1988), writer, filmmaker, director, producer, educator

Lee Daniels, screenwriter, director, executive producer

F. Gary Gray, director, producer, actor

Bill Gunn aka William Harrison Gunn (1934-1989), playwright, screenwriter, director, actor

Will Packer, executive producer, producer, screenwriter

Jordan Peele, actor, screenwriter, executive producer, director

Brock Peters aka George Fisher (1927-2005), actor, singer, executive producer

Wendell Pierce, actor, soundtrack, producer, book author

Lena Waithe, television and screenwriter, executive producer, actor

LIST OF HIP HOP/RAP MOVIES
(Select)

(Film content with hip hop/rap theme)

Wild Style (1983)

Breakin' (1984)

Beat Street (1984)

Breakin' 2: Electric Boogaloo (1984)

Rappin' (1985)

Krush Groove (1985)

House Party (1990)

Boyz n the Hood (1991)

House Party 2 (1991)

Class Act (1992)

Juice (1992)

CB4 (1993)

Fear of a Black Hat (1993)

Menace II Society (1993)

Who's the Man? (1993)

Above the Rim (1994)

Fresh (1994)

House Party 3 (1994)

New Jersey Drive (1995)

I Got the Hook-Up (1998)

Ride (1998)

Slam (1998)

Belly (1998)

Thicker than Water (1999)

Freestyle: The Art of Rhyme (2000)

Bones (2001)

Brooklyn Babylon (2001)

Carmen: A Hip Hopera (2001, Television Movie)

Scratch (2001)

Wave Twisters (2001, Animation)

Ali G Indahouse (2002, British)

Biggie & Tupac (2002)

Brown Sugar (2002)

8 Mile (2002)

Love and a Bullet (2002)

Anne B. Real (2003)

Cradle 2 the Grave (2003)

Death of a Dynasty (2003)

Honey (2003)

Malibu's Most Wanted (2003)

Tupac: Resurrection (2003)

Fade to Black (2004)

Soul Plane (2004)

You Got Served (2004)

Dave Chappelle's Block Party (2005)

Get Rich or Die Tryin' (2005)

Hustle & Flow (2005)

Just for Kicks (2005, Documentary)

ATL (2006)

Save the Last Dance 2 (2006)

Step Up (2006)

Feel the Noise (2007)

1 More Hit (2007)

Stomp the Yard (2007)

Rome & Jewel (2008)

Step Up 2: The Streets (2008)

The Wackness (2008)

The Carter (2009)

A Day In The Life (2009)

A Family Underground (2009)

Janky Promoters (2009)

Notorious (2009)

Coz OV Moni (Ghanaian, 2010)

Hamilius: Hip Hop Culture in Luxembourg (English subtitle, 2010)

Step Up 3D (2010)

Stomp the Yard 2: Homecoming (2010)

StreetDance 3D (the United Kingdom, 2010)

Zeitenändern dich (Time You Change, German, 2010)

Beat the World (2011)

Beats, Rhymes & Life: The Travels of A Tribe Called Quest (2011)

Honey 2 (2011)

Saigon Electric (Vietnamese, English subtitle, 2011)

Let It Shine (Television Movie, 2012)

Something from Nothing: The Art of Rap (2012)

Step Up Revolution (2012)

StreetDance 2 (The United Kingdom, 2012)

You Are God (2012, Polish)

ABCD: Anybody Can Dance (2013, India)

Caught on Tape (2013)

Coz OV Moni 2 (Ghanaian, subtitled, 2013)

Our Vinyl Weighs a Ton: This Is Stones Throw Records (2013)

Nas: Time Is Illmatic (2014)

Step Up: All In (2014)

Top Five (2014)

Born to Dance (2015, New Zealand)

Dope (2015)

Straight Outta Compton (2015)

Stretch and Bobbito: Radio That Changed Lives (2015)

Bad Rap (2016, Asian Documentary)

Morris From America (2016)

Popstar: Never Stop Never Stopping (2016)

All Eyez on Me (2017)

Bodied (2017)

Love Beats Rhymes (2017)

Meesaya Murukku (2017, India)

Patti Cakes$ (2017)

Roxanne Roxanne (Television movie, 2017)

Blindspotting (2018)

Lakshmi (Indian, English subtitle, 2018)

Beats (2019)

Gully Boy (Indian Hindi-language, 2019)

Queen & Slim (2019)

Bibliography
Books

Beachum, Floyd D., McCray, Carlos R. *Cultural Collision and Collusion: Reflections on Hip-hop Culture, Values, and Schools.* New York: Peter Lang Publishing, 2011

Burns, Kate. *Rap Music and Culture.* Farmington Hills, MI: Greenhaven Press, 2008.

Chang, Jeff. *Can't Stop Won't Stop, A History of the Hip-hop Generation.* New York: St. Martin's Press, 2005.

Charnas, Dan. *The Big Payback: The History of the Business of Hip-hop.* New York: New American Library, 2010.

Garofoli, Wendy. *Hip-Hop History.* Minnesota: Capstone Press, 2010

Jackson II, Ronald L., and Richardson, Elaine B. *Understanding African American Rhetoric: Classical Origins to Contemporary Innovations.* New York: Routledge, 2003.

Light, Alan. *The Vibe History of Hip Hop.* New York: Three Rivers Press, 1999.

Monteyne, Kimberly. *Hip Hop on Film: Performance, Culture, Urban Space and Genre Transformation in the 1980s.* Mississippi: University Press of Mississippi, 2013.

Nelson, George. *Hip Hop America.* New York: Penguin Group, 1998.

Nickson, Chris. *Hey Ya! The Unauthorized Biography of OutKast.*

New York: St. Martin's Press, 2004.

Sullivan, Denise. *Keep on Pushing: Black Power Music From Blues to Hip-hop*. Chicago, Illinois: Chicago Review Press, 2011

Websites

https://musicianguide.com/biographies/

http://thesource.com

https://informationcradle.com/

https://www.kidzworld.com/

https://www.famousafricanamericans.org/

https://austinemedia.com/l

player.listenlive.co/22621/en/artist/16_0638ba22-040f-438d83a5.../biography

https://wealthygorilla.com/

https://austinemedia.com/

http://www.hiphopscriptures.com

https://hip-hop-music.fandom.com/wiki/

https://www.grammy.com/grammys/artists/

https://www.oldies.com/artist-biography/

https://www.vice.com/

https://www.last.fm

https://www.notablebiographies.com/

https://www.aarp.org/entertainment/music/info-2019/hip-hop.html

https://www.britannica.com/biography

https://www.thefamouspeople.com/profiles/

https://www.encyclopedia.com/education/news-wires-white-papers-and-books/ (Jan 2019)

https://en.wikipedia.org/

https://www.capitalxtra.com/artists/

https://www.allmusic.com/

https://www.aceshowbiz.com/

www.biography.com

https://www.blackpast.org/african-american-history/people-african-american-history/nipsey-hussle-1985-2019/

www.liveabout.com › Music › Rap & Hip Hop

www.ebony.com

https://achievement.org/

https://www.last.fm/music/

https://www.nypl.org/

https://variety.com/

Breakfast Club Power 105.1 FM

Cherie Johnson Podcast-10/2020

https://www.2pac.com/us/biography

https://hiphopdx.com/

Index

André 3000 3

Big Boi 3

Big Daddy Kane 4

Big Pun 5

Biz Markie 5

Black Thought 5

Busta Rhymes 6

Cam'ron 7

Childish Gambino 7

Common 8

Da Brat 9

David Banner 10

DJ Pooh 10

DMX 11

Doctor Dré 11

Doug E. Fresh 12

Dr. Dre 12

Drake 13

Eminem 14

Eve 15

Fab 5 Freddy 15

Fat Joe 16

The Fat Boys 17

50 Cent 17

Fredro Starr 18

Fresh Prince 19

The Game 21

Ice Cube 21

Ice-T 22

Ja Rule 23

Jay-Z 24

Jim Jones 25

Kid 'n Play 26

Lauryn Hill 27

Lil' Bow Wow aka Bow Wow 27

Lil' Kim 28

Lil' Romeo aka Romeo 29

Lil' Wayne 29

L.L. Cool J 30

Ed Lover 31

Ludacris 31

Marky Mark	32
Master P.	34
MC Hammer	36
MC Lyte	36
Method Man	37
Mos Def	38
Nas	39
Nicki Minaj	40
Nipsey Hussle	41
Pras Michel	42
Puff Daddy aka P. Diddy	42
Q-Tip	44
Queen Latifah	45
RZA	46
Snoop Dogg	47
T.I.	49
Treach	50
Tupac	50
Wyclef Jean	51
Xzibit	52
YoYo	53

www.ingramcontent.com/pod-product-compliance
Lightning Source LLC
Chambersburg PA
CBHW071840290426
44109CB00017B/1876